A History of Resistance
in Namibia

Apartheid & Society

Endgame in
South Africa?

ROBIN COHEN
Co-published with Unesco

Race, Class
& the Apartheid State

HAROLD WOLPE
Co-published with OAU and Unesco

A History of Resistance
in Namibia

PETER H. KATJAVIVI
Co-published with OAU and Unesco

A History of Resistance in Namibia

PETER H. KATJAVIVI

Africa World Press, Inc.
P.O. Box 1892
Trenton, New Jersey 08607

James Currey
London

OAU
Inter-African Cultural Fund · Addis Ababa

Unesco Press
Paris

Africa World Press, Inc.
P.O. Box 1892
Trenton, NJ 08607

First American edition 1990

Library of Congress Catalog Card Number: 89-81236

ISBN: 0-86543-143-4 Cloth
　　　 0-86543-144-2 Paper

CONTENTS

Contents

LIST OF ILLUSTRATIONS

LIST OF MAPS

PREFACE

A History of Resistance in Namibia is part of the Unesco series 'Apartheid and Society'. The first in this series, *Endgame in South Africa?* by Robin Cohen was published in 1986. *A History of Resistance in Namibia* is intended to familiarise the general public with the Namibian issue.

Namibia has received less attention in academic literature than has South Africa. Nevertheless, it presents a number of features which it has in common with South Africa. Colonised first by the Germans, Namibia suffered the wide-scale land alienation that has marked colonial territories of white settlement. Placed under South African trusteeship by the League of Nations, it has further suffered from the apartheid policies of a South Africa anxious to treat Namibia as if incorporated into the Republic. While this process has partly been halted, the status of Walvis Bay, the continuing South African armed occupation of Namibia and the continuing racial and ethnic segregation all raise real questions as to South Africa's intentions with regard to a country rich in mineral wealth and the centre of lucrative Karakul and fishing industries. In any event, South Africa has consistently refused the free democratic elections under United Nations supervision repeatedly demanded by General Assembly resolutions.

Colonisation and occupation, land alienation and 'Bantu Education' have not, however, been imposed on a docile Namibia. This book traces not so much the history of domination as that of African resistance. This resistance has always existed. Resisting in culture and religion in some epochs, through strike action and boycotts in others, Africans have united across clan boundaries to demand an end to apartheid and to struggle for complete independence.

This struggle by Africans has not been a simple unilinear one. It has in itself been affected by the complexities of African organisations, old and new forms of stratification, by differences in strategies and by differing coalitions.

Publication of *A History of Resistance in Namibia* marks the 21st anniversary of the passing of Resolution 2145 (XXI) of 27 October 1966, by which the UN General Assembly terminated the mandate that had placed Namibia under South African trusteeship. The ideas and opinions it expresses are, however, those of the author and do not necessarily represent the views of Unesco.

INTRODUCTION

Namibia is one of Africa's least known countries. To some it is the former German South West Africa; to others a unique case in international law. It is the last African country still fighting for independence from European rule and it suffers a unique form of domination – occupation by South Africa. The people of Namibia share with the people of South Africa an experience of the racist system of apartheid that has also been extended to Namibia. The Namibian liberation struggle led by SWAPO – the South West Africa People's Organisation – has to combat the military might of the white minority regime in South Africa and its attempts to dominate the whole southern African region.

What, then, is SWAPO? Who are the people of Namibia? What is it that has shaped their identity and brought different communities together in opposition to foreign rule? This book attempts to answer these questions and traces the history of Namibian resistance to both German and South African domination.

I should like to thank Unesco for contracting this study and encouraging me to complete it as a broad-based historical account of Namibian resistance. Such an account, however brief, is overdue.

Very little is known about the Namibian past and what has been written has been heavily distorted. I also strongly believe those who say that in order for us to understand the present we must understand the past. Thus, this account attempts to provide a historical perspective. It is hoped that in this way the book will provide the reader with a panoramic setting of Namibian resistance, as traced from primary resistance against colonial rule to the fully-fledged armed liberation struggle of today. I try to show how successive Namibian generations have continued to resist German and South African domination, and thereby place the contemporary struggle in the context of the general opposition conducted by Namibian communities to foreign rule.

It is to end the agony described in this book that the Namibian people are today locked in a bitter struggle against the South African regime, in order to be able freely to determine their political destiny.

Peter H Katjavivi
Oxford

LIST OF ACRONYMS

AFM	Armed Forces Movement
AIS	African Improvement Society
AKTUR	Action Front for the Retention of Turnhalle Principles
AME	African Methodist Episcopal church
ANC	African National Congress
CANU	Caprivi African National Union
DEMKOP	Democratic Co-operative Party
DTA	Democratic Turnhalle Alliance
DUF	Damara United Front
ELK	Evangelical Lutheran church
ELOK	Evangelical Lutherian Ovambo-Kavango church
FCWU	Food and Canning Workers' Union
FLN	National Liberation Front (Algeria)
FNL	National Liberation Front (Vietnam)
FNLA	National Front for the Liberation of Angola
FRELIMO	Front for the Liberation of Mozambique
ICJ	International Court of Justice
MPLA	Popular Movement for the Liberation of Angola
NACIP	Namib Convention Independence Party
NAPDO	Namib African People's Organisation
NC	National Convention
NCN	National Convention of Namibia
NNC	Namibia National Convention
NNF	Namibia National Front
NUDO	National Unity Democratic Organisation
OAU	Organisation of African Unity
OPC	Ovamboland People's Congress
OPO	Ovamboland People's Organisation
PLAN	People's Liberation Army of Namibia
PROSWA	Pro-South West Africa Foundation
SADF	South African Defence Force
SWADU	South West Africa Democratic Union
SWANLA	South West Africa Native Labour Association
SWANLIF	South West Africa National Liberation Front
SWANU	South West Africa National Union
SWAPA	South West Africa Progressive Association

SWAPDUF	South West Africa People's Democratic United Front
SWAPO	South West Africa People's Organisation
SWAPO-D	SWAPO-Democrats
SWASB	South West Africa Student Body
SWANIO	South West Africa United National Independence Organisation
SWATF	South West Africa Territory Force
SYL	SWAPO Youth League
UN or UNO	United Nations Organisation
UNESCO	United Nations Educational, Scientific and Cultural Organisation
UNIA	Universal Negro Improvement Association
UNIP	Unitede National Independence Party
UNIN	United Nations Institute for Namibia
UNIPP	United Namib Independence People's Party
UNITA	National Union for the Total Independence of Angola
UNTAG	UN Transitional Assistance Group
VOSWA	Volks-Organizasie van Suidwes Afrika
ZANU	Zimbabwe African National Union
ZAPU	Zimbabwe African People's Union

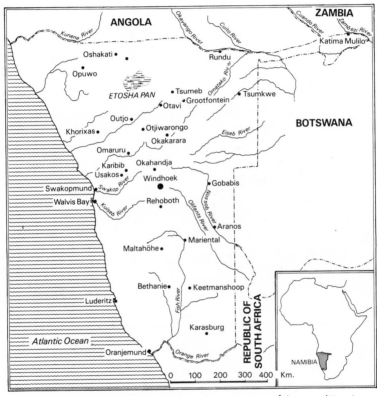

1 & 2 Namibia in Africa and main towns and intermittent rivers

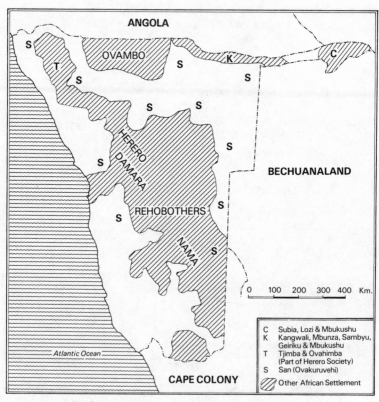

ANGOLA

OVAMBO

S

T

S

S

K

C

S

S

S

HERERO
DAMARA

S

S

BECHUANALAND

REHOBOTHERS

S

S

NAMA

S

S

0   100   200   300   400   Km.

C   Subia, Lozi & Mbukushu
K   Kangwali, Mbunza, Sambyu,
    Geiriku & Mbukushu
T   Tjimba & Ovahimba
    (Part of Herero Society)
S   San (Ovakuruvehi)
    Other African Settlement

Atlantic Ocean

CAPE COLONY

3   *Areas of African settlement, 1900*

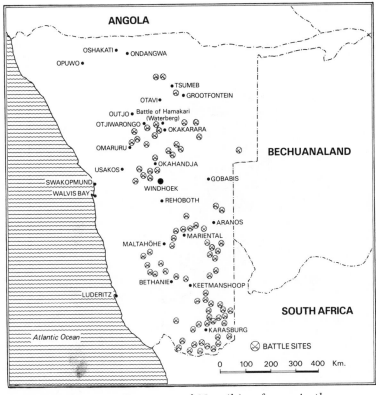

4 Battles between German and Namibian forces in the
1904–7 War

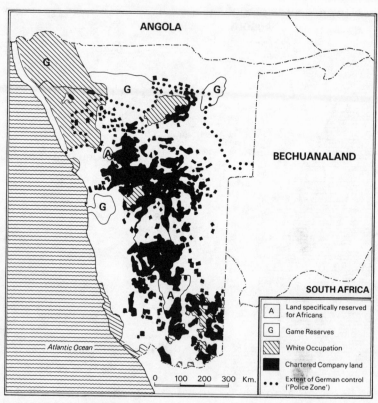

ANGOLA

G

G

G

BECHUANALAND

A

SOUTH AFRICA

G

A

Atlantic Ocean

A	Land specifically reserved for Africans
G	Game Reserves
	White Occupation
	Chartered Company land
•••	Extent of German control ('Police Zone')

0 100 200 300 Km.

5 *Settlement, 1911*

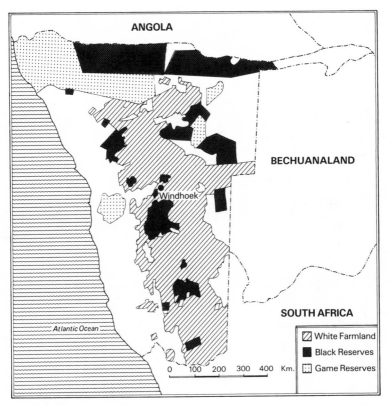

6   Settlement, 1937

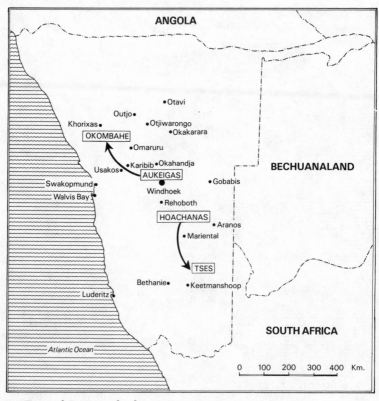

7 Forced Removals, late 1950s (see page 47)

8 Settlement proposed under the Odendaal Plan

ANGOLA

Katima Mulilo

Oshakati
Ondangwa
Rundu

Tsumeb
Otavi Grootfontein
Tsumkwe

Outjo
Khorixas
Otjiwarongo Okakarara

Omaruru
Karibib
Okahandja

BECHUANALAND

Swakopmund
Walvis Bay
Usakos Windhoek
Gobabis
Rehoboth

Maltahöhe
Mariental

Luderitz
Bethanie
Keetmanshoop

Atlantic Ocean

REPUBLIC OF
SOUTH AFRICA

0   100   200   300   400 Km.

1	KAOKOVELD
2	OVAMBOLAND
3	OKAVANGOLAND
4	EAST CAPRIVI
5	DAMARALAND
6	BUSHMANLAND
7	HEREROLAND
8	REHOBOTH
9	TSWANALAND
10	NAMALAND

GAME RESERVES

9 Main South African military bases, operational area

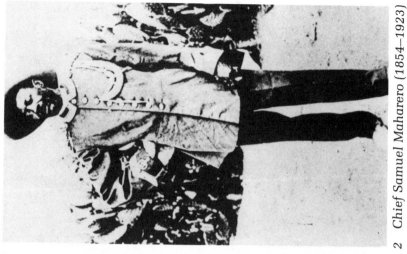

1 Chief Maharero (1820–90)

2 Chief Samuel Maharero (1854–1923)

4 *Namibian prisoners held by the Germans during the 1904–7 war*

3 *Chief Hendrik Witbooi (1840–1905)*

5 Jacob Marenga and his lieutenants

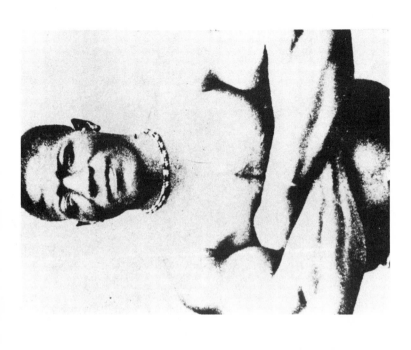

6 Chief Mandume (c.1890–1917)

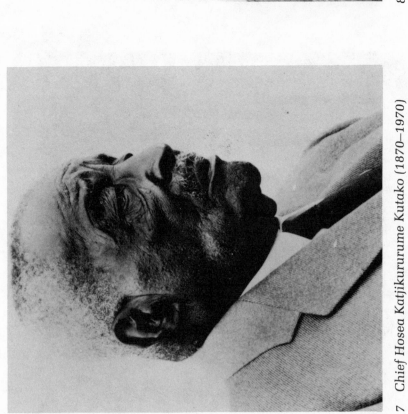

7 Chief Hosea Katjikururume Kutako (1870–1970)

8 SWAPO Founder, and now SWAPO
   Secretary-General, Andimba Ja Toivo

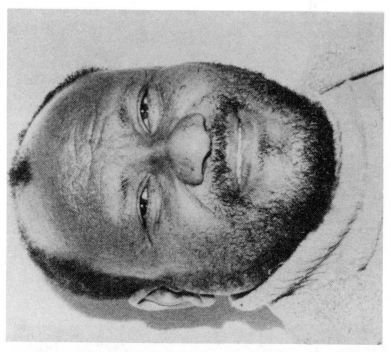

10 Gerson Hitjevi Veii, ex-Robben Island prisoner, SWANU President from 1968 to 1982, and now head of SWANU's political bureau

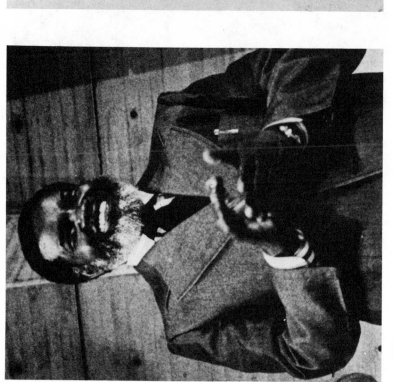

9 SWAPO President Sam Nujoma

11 SWAPO fighters

12 Peter Nanyemba, (1935–83) SWAPO Secretary for
Defence

13   Units of the South African armed forces deployed in Namibia

14   South African helicopters and helicopter gunships in use in Namibia

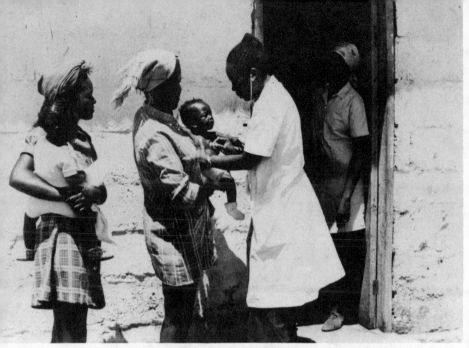

15 Dr Libertine Inaaviposa Amathila, SWAPO Deputy-Secretary for Health and Welfare, at the clinic in the Nyango Health and Education Centre, Zambia, run by SWAPO

16 SWAPO supporters in Namibia, 1978

1 NAMIBIA UP TO THE 1860s

In spite of German and South African land expropriations, the pattern of African settlement in Namibia today generally reflects that of the pre-colonial era. The Herero and Damara people lived in central and north-western parts of the territory, while in the north were the Ovambo communities, extending into what is now southern Angola. Various Nama clans were settled in southern Namibia, the Orlams migrating from the Cape during the early nineteenth century. The Rehobothers (also originally from the Cape) established their community south of Windhoek in 1870. In Okavango there were five groups of people – the Kangwali, Mbunza, Sambyu, Mbukushu and Geiriku. The Mbukushu also extended into Caprivi, alongside Subia and Lozi people. Groups from both Okavango and Caprivi were not, however, confined to territory within the current borders of Namibia but were part of wider societies that crossed these borders.

The oldest inhabitants of Namibia, as of the rest of southern Africa, are the nomadic San. They are often referred to as 'Bushmen' but I prefer to use the Herero word 'Ovakuruvehi', meaning 'the ancient (or original) ones'. Today the Ovakuruvehi of Namibia mostly live along the Kalahari desert and in the Grootfontein area. Modern technology, other cultures and economic and political pressures have affected their lifestyle, but in many ways it remains much the same as it has been for centuries. These people have always been skilled hunter-gatherers, finding food and water in areas where others could not survive. They lived in small autonomous communities that did not have permanent settlements but moved around within a certain broad area, following the search for food. They shared a common language group and general cultural characteristics, although there were distinct differences between the various groups.

The Hereros were pastoralists, their economic base being the rearing of cattle. The Damaras and Namas also lived on the produce of cattle, goats and sheep, and the Damaras were skilled hunters. The various Ovambo communities, however, were mostly cultivators and agriculturalists. Those communities living nearer the coast, and those in Okavango and Caprivi, caught and ate fish. Others supplemented their diet by collecting wild berries and nuts.

These were separate societies with different cultures and areas of settlement, often demarcated by rivers or other geographical features. But they interacted with each other considerably. Groups from the different societies would sometimes live alongside each other, and there was a certain amount of trading between them. This was an exchange of commodities that one or another community lacked, such as cattle, goats, salt, tools, wooden bowls and utensils, pots, skins (for mats and blankets), plus ornaments such as ostrich feathers and shells. The Ovambos and Damaras were also known for their copper smelting.

The political structures of the different societies also varied. However, they did share certain characteristics as far as they related to the question of land. The life of each society revolved around the land and its use. Individual wealth derived from proper utilisation of the land, although in most cases people did not own or possess land as such. As people lived communally, those who did not possess cattle or were not able to produce food through cultivation of the land, for one reason or another, were provided for within the community.

The Nama communities were originally based on five or six clans which claimed rights to specific areas and waterholes, although they were not separated on strict territorial grounds. The settlements were fairly large, numbering between 800 and 1,500 people each. Food and shelter were provided by the women. Cattle raising and herding and occasional hunting were traditionally men's activities. In the early nineteenth century Orlam groups began to migrate north across the Orange River from the Cape. At first they settled amongst the Namas, but as their numbers grew they competed with the Namas for grazing land and water and conflict between the two communities developed between 1820 and 1830. This was eventually settled by an agreement between the main Orlam leader, Jonker Afrikaner, and Oasib, a senior Nama leader, which allowed both communities to share equal rights in the area of southern Namibia. The Jonker Afrikaner group won control of the area east of Windhoek and north of the Kuiseb river, however, and became the most powerful group in that part of the country.

Jonker Afrikaner once told some European explorers that the Damaras had 'always existed' in Namibia.[1] He claimed that they used to live across a broad area of central Namibia, but increasingly took refuge in the mountainous regions as the Hereros took over more land in their search for grazing lands

2

for their cattle. They are a community about which little is written, and what there is tends to portray a picture of a scattered group of people dominated by the Namas and Hereros. In fact, however, Damara settlements were stable ones and included copper mining and working.[2] They share a common language group and some cultural characteristics with the Namas and, by the early nineteenth century, lived alongside and interacted closely with both Nama and Herero societies.

The central part of Namibia (from Windhoek up to Otavi) was populated by Hereros. They formed fairly separate communities, linked by language and culture, but based on the family/clan unit, without any unified chieftaincy system. Oral history and anthropological evidence suggests that Herero-speaking communities first came to Namibia from central/east Africa in the sixteenth century and settled in Kaokoveld, where the Herero-speaking Ovahimba and Ovatjimba still live today. It was not until the eighteenth century that some of them moved southwards, eventually being checked by the Orlam community under Jonker Afrikaner. By the 1870s, Windhoek (Otjomuise) was considered to be part of Hereroland.

These communities were rich in cattle, some chiefs possessing 'such enormous herds as to arouse the admiration and envy of more than one European contemporary, especially in the latter part of the 19th century'.[3] Their settlements were semi-permanent and there was some trading with the Ovambo communities to the north, especially in iron and copper articles.

The various Ovambo communities in the north of Namibia were made up of seven groups with different but associated languages and shared common cultural characteristics. They possessed some cattle and a few sheep. The main means of subsistence, however, was cultivation on the fertile river plains, although this was a small area for a large population. Corn, millet, maize, beans, groundnuts and pumpkins were grown. In these societies the chiefs exercised greater control over their subjects than in the rest of the country. The family was, however, the unit of production, with men being responsible for stock herding, heavy agricultural work and most crafts. Women were responsible for cultivation, fishing, domestic work and a few crafts.[4]

These were not static societies existing in a fixed form for hundreds of years. Nor did they always peacefully co-exist. But conflict did not always run on ethnic lines as some colonial writers would have us believe. Rather, it was the product of wider socio-economic changes. The internal dynamics of these societies interacted with external stimuli for change, in the form of increasing trade and contact with Europeans. Thus the migration of the Orlams north into Namibia at the beginning of the nineteenth century was in response to pressures from European expansion in the Cape. This in turn put pressure on grazing lands and water supplies in southern Namibia. The process of accommodation of Orlam groups by the Nama clans, with attendant conflict, broke down traditional Nama social structures. A new form of social and economic organisation emerged – the kommando.[5] It was a smaller unit than the old Nama groups and was essentially 10–50 men around a family leader, using horses and guns acquired through trade with the Cape to raid the cattle and possessions of other communities.

In the mid-nineteenth century the Orlams under Jonker Afrikaner and various Nama groups came increasingly into conflict with the Hereros, over land, cattle and water rights. This developed into a prolonged war between the Namas and Hereros that lasted until a treaty was signed between them in 1870. Sporadic fighting broke out again in the early 1880s, but by this time there were the new problems caused by German intervention in Namibia. In the process of these wars Hendrik Witbooi emerged as a leading Nama figure and asserted his authority over many other Nama groups.

The late nineteenth century also saw the rise of a central Herero chieftaincy, under Maharero and his son Samuel Maharero. This came about through four main processes. First, intermarriage between the major family 'houses' put Maharero in a strong position of authority over other Herero chiefs. Second, Maharero became a unifying leader in the wars with the Orlams and their leader Jonker Afrikaner. Third, the Germans were keen to promote one central Herero leader with whom they could seek and sign treaties, as they did with both Maharero (1885) and Samuel Maharero (1894). Fourth, Samuel Maharero used the 1896 rebellion against German rule as an opportunity to strengthen his own position, by joining the Germans in quelling it. (See chapter 2.)

Social stratification also intensified in the Ovambo communities in the nineteenth century, and one account describes a feudal class structure already emerging by the middle of the century.[6] The ruling group exacted tribute from occupiers of land and a form of slavery developed. This was partly due to

the expanding consumer desires of the kings and their lenga war leaders, which could not be met merely by raiding. An increasingly oppressive tax burden thus fell upon the shoulders of commoners, and a stratum of men who had lost their cattle emerges.[7]

EARLY EUROPEAN PENETRATION

The first recorded arrival of Europeans in Namibia was when the Portuguese sailor and explorer Diogo Cao landed at Cape Cross in 1485. All he saw was the endless sands of the famous Namib desert; he did not encounter any people from the Namibian communities living beyond the desert or in the Swakop river valley. In 1486, another Portuguese explorer, Bartholomew Diaz, sailed round the Cape before heading back to Portugal. He stopped and erected a stone cross at a place he named Angra Pequena, near the present town of Luderitz. He also reported seeing some Africans and large herds of cattle in the area of the Fish river.[8]

After these two landings, no Europeans came to Namibia until the seventeenth century. Then in the 1670s Dutch explorers from the Cape landed in Namibia and initiated the first face-to-face encounters between Europeans and Africans. It was not until the late 1700s, however, that European influence and some early settlers really began to penetrate Namibia.

Around 1793 some Cape-based Dutch settlers moved into Namibia, even as far north as Grootfontein, and established themselves as farmers. Then when the Orlams migrated into Namibia in the early nineteenth century they opened up the south of the country to trade routes with the Cape. This brought guns and some European-made goods into Namibia. The first European traders actually to come to Namibia themselves did so in the late eighteenth century but these were few in number and their activities were low-key. By the mid-nineteenth century the number of traders had increased and their network extended as far north as Etosha. They were still small-scale entrepreneurs, but they introduced firearms into Namibia, thus making any conflict between Namibian communities much worse.

Early European penetration mainly consisted of such traders, plus missionaries and explorers. Indeed, it was a Swedish explorer, Charles John Andersson, who travelled in 1856 through central and northern parts of Namibia, and later coined the name by which the territory came to be known, 'South West Africa'. Previously it had been referred to as the Trans-Gariep

5

('across the Orange River', Gariep being the old Nama name for the Orange) but more often by region only, in terms of the local communities, as Namaqualand, Damaraland and Ovamboland. Other key explorers in the mid-nineteenth century were Galton, Baines, Green and Chapman.

Missionary activity was spearheaded by the London Missionary Society and the Wesleyans, who began to operate in Namibia in 1802, in the south of the country. They were followed, from 1840 onwards, by German and then Finnish Lutheran missionaries. One of the principal Lutherans was the German Hugo Hahn, who established the first settled Lutheran mission at Otjikango, near Okahandja, in 1844 and his first trip to Ovamboland was in 1857.

The missionaries, in particular those of the German Rhenish Lutheran Mission, believed in their own 'civilising' mission, which centred on the promotion of European culture as much as on the Bible message itself. The Director of the Rhenish Missionary Society in the late nineteenth century, F. Fabri, saw mission work as 'useful' for trade or colonial annexation and one particular missionary, C G Buttner, 'strove zealously to promote German colonial government in South West Africa'.[9] When German colonial rule was formally established, many missionaries therefore took cover under it, and on the whole they kept silent about German brutalities in Namibia and the harsh regime later imposed by South Africa.

2 GERMAN CONQUEST & NAMIBIAN RESISTANCE

The arrival of increasing numbers of Afrikaner and German settlers and the activities of the traders and missionaries seriously disrupted Namibian societies. Conflict between the Namas and Hereros over cattle and grazing land was made worse with the advent of guns sold by traders, and this led to the Herero chief, Maharero, signing a treaty with the British in 1876. This was supposed to offer the Herero people protection from their enemies. Then in 1876 Britain annexed the area around Walvis Bay.

In 1883–4 the German businessman Adolf Luderitz came to an agreement, after lengthy negotiations with Chief Joseph Frederick of Bethanie, which gave him the rights over the area around Angra Pequena. The settlement was soon renamed Luderitz. This opened up the country to German economic and political interests and the formal establishment of German colonial rule in the country.

In trying to establish control over Namibia the Germans relied upon the use of force and the old colonial tactics of divide and rule. They tried to play Namibian groups off against each other, using competition over land and cattle to divide them, or forced them to sign protection treaties giving away their land. Thus in 1885 Herero Chief Maharero agreed a protection treaty with the Germans which allocated an ill-defined area for European settlement. But the German expropriation of land and cattle caused Maharero to break off the treaty in 1888. The first German Commissioner, Dr H.E. Göring, (father of the Nazi War Minister Hermann Göring) was forced to retreat to Walvis Bay. It was then that the first contingent of German troops was sent to Namibia, under Captain von Francois, to secure the area for Germany once again.

Von Francois tried to lay down specific borders to Hereroland and moved his troops to Windhoek to create a buffer zone between the Namas and Hereros. Then in 1890 Maharero died and the German colonial authorities and missionaries supported the claim of his son, Samuel Maharero (a Christian), in the succession, although the first in line was actually Nikodemus Kambahahiza Kavikunua, son of Maharero's older brother and a chief of the eastern Hereros. In 1896, Kambahahiza and

Kahimemua, another prominent Herero chief, openly rebelled against the continuing German encroachment of their land. Samuel Maharero saw this as a challenge to his own authority and sided with the Germans in quelling the rebellion. Kambahahiza and Kahimemua were executed and the cattle of the eastern Hereros were expropriated.

In the south of Namibia, Hendrik Witbooi had, by the 1880s, become a strong military figure and leading Nama chief. He had won this position through raids on other Nama clans and on Herero settlements, taking their cattle, horses and other livestock. But in the early 1890s he increasingly attacked German encampments and supply convoys. The new German governor, Leutwein, subdued the smaller Nama clans by force in 1894, taking their horses so that they could not mount such effective resistance to the German troops. He covered southern Namibia with a network of small military posts, building up to a large-scale attack on Witbooi in August 1894, after which Witbooi was forced to sign a treaty with the Germans.

THE 1904–7 WAR OF RESISTANCE

Eventually, such tactics led to a widespread war of resistance to German rule by the Nama and Herero people, from 1904 to 1907. In a letter to the German governor, Leutwein, Herero Chief Samuel Maharero described the killings that were the immediate cause of the war:

> It has been started by the Whites (yourself). You yourself know how many Hereros have been killed by White people, particularly traders with guns, and in prisons, and whenever I took these matters to Windhoek the blood of my people was compensated for by a small number of small stock . . . Lieutenant Z . . . started killing my people in gaol. There died (were killed) 10 . . . In the end he placed and secreted in the fort soldiers (from the Civilian Reserve) and he called me in order to shoot me . . . [he] sent men with guns in order to shoot me. Thereupon I became angry and said – 'now I must shoot the Whites even though I die' . . . Thus the war commenced.[1]

On 12 January 1904 the Hereros declared war on the Germans. Samuel Maharero ordered that no women, children, unarmed or non-German Europeans were to be attacked. Efforts were made to bring the Namas and Rehobothers into the uprising as well, but a key letter sent from Samuel Maharero to

Nama Chief Hendrik Witbooi was taken by the Germans. It contained the following call:

> All our patience with the Germans is of little avail, for each day they shoot someone dead for no reason at all. Hence I appeal to you, my brother, not to hold aloof from the uprising, but to make your voice heard so that all Africa may take up arms against the Germans. Let us die fighting rather than die as a result of maltreatment, imprisonment or some other calamity. Tell all the Kapteins [chiefs] down there to rise and do battle.[2]

The Namas did join the uprising in October 1904. Indeed, most of the communities in central and southern Namibia – Damaras, Hereros and most of the Nama groups including the Bondelswarts – took part in the uprising. The Rehobothers did not. The Ovambo communities to the north were not directly involved because they had generally not been brought under German control, but they did aid people fleeing from German retribution in the rest of the country.

When war was declared by Samuel Maharero, Leutwein and most of the German troops were in the south of the country quelling an uprising by the Bondelswarts. In their absence, the Hereros were able to seize control of much of the central part of the country. Over 100 German men – settlers and soldiers – were killed; railway and telegraphic links were destroyed and so were some German farms, although the families were spared.[3] German garrisons and settlements were beseiged. For six months the Hereros held their positions. Then the Germans brought in troop reinforcements and a new military head – General Von Trotha – who had brutally repressed African resistance to German rule in East Africa.

On 11 August 1904 the decisive battle was fought at Hamakari, east of Otjozondjupa (Waterberg). Herero men, women and children were camped there together and encircled by German troops. Thousands were killed. Some broke through German lines to the east and were followed and forced into the Kalahari desert, where many more died. Others managed to flee northwards and were aided, in particular, by Chief Nehale of the Ondonga community. Others still sought refuge elsewhere in the country. But many were taken as prisoners of war and used as slave labour on the railways, where there were more deaths.

In October 1904 Von Trotha issued an extermination order, declaring that inside German territory every Herero tribesman, armed or unarmed, with or without cattle, will be shot. No women and children will be allowed in the territory: they will be driven back to their people or fired upon . . . I believe that the Herero must be destroyed as a nation.[4]

By the end of 1905, 75–80% of the Herero population had been killed, reduced from 60,000–80,000 to some 16,000. Of these, 14,000 were in German concentration camps.[5] Others had fled to South Africa or across the Kalahari desert into Botswana, where their descendants live today.

In October 1904 the Namas, under the leadership of Chief Hendrik Witbooi, took up arms against the Germans and shifted the focus of the war to the south of the country. Witbooi himself was killed in action in October 1905 and some Nama groups, dispirited by this loss, surrendered. But guerrilla bands, under leaders such as Abraham Morris, Jacob Marenga (whose name has often been misspelt as Marengo), Cornelius, Johannes Christian and Simon Kopper, continued to fight the German troops until 1907–8. Jacob Marenga was renowned as a successful guerrilla leader and in 1907 the then German Governor, Bruno von Schuckmann, reported that an appearance by Marenga in Namibia was 'like an electric shock, causing great excitement among the natives, all the way to the north'.[6] Marenga was eventually followed by British and German troops acting together and was killed in the Cape in September 1907. Simon Kopper was based for some time in Botswana, and mounted raids across the border into Namibia. Here again the British co-operated with the Germans. They offered him land on which to settle in Botswana if he stopped his guerrilla resistance to German rule in Namibia. Kopper accepted and he and a small group of followers settled in Botswana.

The Namas also suffered dreadfully in the war of resistance. By 1911, 35–50% of the Nama population had been killed; it was down to 9,800, from an estimated 15,000–20,000 in 1892.[7] Prisoners of war suffered similar hardships to the Hereros. Some were deported to Togo and Cameroon, which were also under German colonial rule then, and many of them died from illness and mistreatment.

The effect of the war on the Namibian communities in central and southern Namibia was devastating. 'It was a catastrophe, caused not only by the effects of war but by German measures during the war and the native policies of the post-war years.'[8] There was a total expropriation of land, a ban on cattle-raising and on traditional forms of organisation. Chiefs and headmen were executed as ringleaders of the uprising. Many Namas and Hereros were deported to other parts of the country.

THE NATURE OF GERMAN COLONIAL RULE

German colonial rule in Namibia had three key elements. First, land was taken from the Namibian people and made available to German settlers. Second, traditional social structures were destroyed to try to make Namibians subservient colonial subjects. Third, Namibians were used as forced labourers on the now white-owned land and the new mines and early industries.

Lands taken from the Namas and Hereros after the war of resistance were given to German settlers and increasing numbers of Germans emigrated to Namibia. By 1911 most of the good land in the centre and south of the country that had previously been in African hands was white-owned (see Map 5).

No education was provided for Namibians by the German colonial regime. The missionaries offered some education, but they were under instructions from the colonial authorities to confine this to teaching the Bible and some German, rather than reading and writing. Herero Chief Frederick Maharero described the German attitudes towards African education as follows:

The Germans fought us and took away our land. That is why they do not want to see any good in us. They converted us to Christianity but did not want to give us any education or to help us to advance. They only preached to us. The Hereros did not learn anything from them except the word 'God'. The Germans were afraid of the Herero people. They did not want them to learn and to become civilised as we want today. I was taken to Germany with the others to be shown to the Kaiser because he did not know his black subjects, and also to be taught . . . We were there one year [about 1894]. We were not taught anything. Only we rode about on horses and dressed and drilled as soldiers.[9]

The Germans never controlled or administered the northern part of Namibia beyond the so-called 'Red Line', south of which was termed the 'Police Zone'. But the north was increasingly used as a source of labour, setting a pattern of forced labour under appalling conditions and poverty-level wages. When Namibians from the centre and south of the country were dispossessed of their land after the 1904–7 war of resistance, they were compelled to work for the Germans by a series of pass and vagrancy laws. But after the Tsumeb copper mine was opened in 1906 and diamond mining started in 1908 around Luderitz, more workers were needed. They were brought from the north of Namibia on fixed-term contracts. By 1910 some 10,000 Ovambo contract workers were already coming south to work, mostly on the mines and railways.[10]

It was the natural and mineral wealth of Namibia that led to the Germans creating this system of exploitation of Namibian labour and resources. The white wealth and black poverty brought about by this are still the basic features of Namibia today.

3 THE SOUTH AFRICAN TAKE-OVER & THE LEAGUE OF NATIONS MANDATE

During the First World War South African forces, acting at the request of the British Government, invaded Namibia. Generals Botha and Smuts led a force of some 8,000 men, entering the country in January 1915 through Walvis Bay and Luderitz. They advanced on the German colonial forces, which numbered about 9,000, and eventually took control of the capital, Windhoek, on 12 May 1915. A South African military governor, Sir Howard Gorges, was appointed and he ran the country under martial law.

As soon as the war ended in Europe, the Allied Powers convened the Peace Conference which was held in Paris in 1919. The desire to prevent another outbreak of war on such a scale led to the formation of the League of Nations and this was also seen as an appropriate body for dealing with the former German colonies. South Africa, acting on behalf of Britain, was made responsible for Namibia under the terms of a League of Nations Mandate. This was signed in Geneva on 17 December 1920 and came into effect on 1 January 1921, when the period of South African martial law in Namibia ended.

South Africa was expected, under the terms of the mandate, to administer Namibia as a 'sacred trust of civilisation'.

> The Mandatory shall promote to the utmost the material and moral well-being, and the social progress of the inhabitants of the Territory ... the Mandatory shall see that the slave trade is prohibited, and that no forced labour is permitted except for essential public works and services, and then only for adequate remuneration.[1]

But it is clear that the intentions of Generals Smuts and Botha, who attended the Paris Conference, had always been to incorporate Namibia fully into the Union of South Africa. Indeed South Africa not only failed to promote the 'material and moral well-being' and 'social progress' of the people of Namibia, but actively set about moulding them into servants of white society. South Africa's record on Namibia has been aptly described as follows:

> As they concerned the South West African natives, the Mandatory Power's administration of justice, its education

policy, its health policy, its land policy, its attitudes towards missions, its attitude towards the prohibition of arms and liquor and towards native affairs in general, all revolved around the basic assumption that the African's existence had only one important purpose – to serve white interests.[2]

THE NATURE OF SOUTH AFRICAN RULE

South Africa continued and extended the land expropriations of the Germans and encouraged more white settlers to come to the country, mostly Afrikaners from South Africa. When they took over control of Namibia there were 1,138 farms in white use. By the end of 1925, 880 holdings had been sold to 1,106 new settlers. By 1926 the white population was almost double that of 1914, even though some 6,000 German soldiers and officials had been repatriated to Germany.[3] The new South African regime went out of its way to assist white settlers with financial loans, and built dams and waterholes for them. A special fund was also set up to encourage Afrikaners who had trekked as far north as Angola in 1874 to come south and settle in Namibia, and many did so.

The other side of this policy of white settlement was the establishment of reserves for the African population. In 1922, the Native Reserves Commission recommended a mere 10% of the land in the centre and south of the country for Africans to live on – 5 million hectares out of 57 million. But the actual proclamation of 1923 was even worse: it gave Africans only 2 million hectares.[4] Yet blacks (Africans and so-called Coloureds) formed 90% of the population.

Namibians in the centre and south of the country were increasingly moved into areas allocated for them – dry sandveld that could not provide adequate grazing for their cattle and other livestock. Many Hereros were moved to reserves at Epukiro and Aminuis, bordering on the Kalahari desert where so many Hereros had died after the battle of Hamakari. At Epukiro, a well had to be driven 800 feet deep before water could be found. By 1937 the white take-over of land in the central and southern regions started by the Germans, was almost total, with the African population confined to small barren reserves (see Map 6). The northern regions were not opened up for white settlement, but the German 'Red Line' was pushed further north, taking land away from the area where over half the African population of Namibia lived.

The reserves and northern regions allocated to Africans have never been able to sustain their populations. This is not accidental. It is a fundamental characteristic of South African policy for they were always intended to be pools of labour from which black workers would come to the so-called white areas – the mines, railways, farms, developing industries, etc. By confining Africans in these areas the South African regime has avoided having to pay wages that would support a black worker and his/her family, and has avoided the costs of proper housing, sanitation, health care and social provision.

A network of rigid laws and regulations has controlled the movement of all black Namibians under South African rule. As early as 1920 a proclamation was issued that made it an offence to be wandering about as an 'idle or a vagrant person, or a person without visible means of support', with any 'offenders' being forced to work for an employer specified by the courts.[5] Together with the various other laws that governed where blacks could live and work, this was a clear policy of forced labour that directly contravened the terms of the League of Nations mandate.

Within the black labour force, South Africa created three distinct groups of workers:

1 Those few Africans qualified to live and therefore work in towns or on white farms. The men worked mostly as messengers and 'shop boys', and later, as some education for Namibians was introduced, as clerks or teachers. The women almost all worked as domestic servants in white homes, although later some trained as nurses and teachers. To this group should also be added the so-called Coloureds and Rehobothers who have residency rights in their own urban areas.

2 Male migrant workers from the reserves in the centre and south of the country, many of whom worked on white farms.

3 Male contract workers from the north, mostly working on the mines, railways and fisheries (in Walvis Bay).

These differentiations have also coincided with ethnic ones – another feature of South Africa's wider approach of divide and rule.

The most exploited group of black workers in Namibia has been the contract workers from the north. Two contract recruiting agencies were established in 1925 – the Southern Recruiting Organisation for the diamond mines, and the Northern Labour Organisation for the Tsumeb copper mine and other employers. In 1943 these merged into the South West Africa Native Labour Association (SWANLA). Men being recruited were given a rudimentary medical check and then divided into three categories of fitness: (a) for work underground in the mines; (b) for surface work on the mines or for heavy farm labour; and (c) for lighter farm work as sheep or cattle herders. No choice was given to the workers. No hours or conditions of work were specified. 'Only the servant is required to render the master his service at all fair and reasonable times.'[6]

4 LAND, LABOUR &
COMMUNITY-BASED RESISTANCE (1920–60)

When the South Africans took over Namibia they prepared a comprehensive account for Britain of the character of German rule. This was made public on 19 January 1918, and was known as the Blue Book on Namibia. In it, the South Africans accused the Germans of

> callous indifference with which she [Germany] treated the guaranteed rights of the native peoples established there, and of the cruelties to which she subjected those people when the burden became too heavy and they attempted to assert their rights.[1]

The South Africans promoted themselves as the liberators of the Namibian people. The commission that prepared the Blue Book took evidence from Namibians of the treatment they had received at the hands of the Germans and created the impression that things would be different under South African rule. Namibians were, moreover, deliberately led to believe that they would recover their lost lands and control over their own affairs. Lord Buxton, Governor-General of South Africa, visited Namibia in 1915 and 'addressed the natives at all important centres and on each occasion promised the Hereros the old freedom along with great possessions of land and unlimited herds of cattle'.[2] Nor was it only the Hereros who expected land to be returned to them:

> From all over the territory the authorities were compelled to listen uneasily to the insistent demand of the Hereros, the Nama clans and the so-called Basters of Rehoboth for the return of lands and privileges usurped by the Germans.[3]

Far from living up to their promises, however, the South Africans took more land from the various Namibian communities.

In the north of the country the Ukuanyama community led by Chief Mandume (then only 21 years old) had fought both against the Portuguese to their north and the South Africans to their south, to try to retain their autonomy. However, after extended battles with the Portuguese in which some 5,000

Africans were killed, Mandume and some of his people were forced to flee south into Namibia. After taking over Namibia from the Germans the South Africans were eager to establish control of the northern part of Namibia and to fix the northern border exactly and they worked with the Portuguese against Mandume. Lieutenant Hahn (who later became the first Native Commissioner for Ovamboland) was sent to demand Mandume's surrender, but the chief refused, saying 'If the English want me, I am here and they can come and fetch me. I will fight till my last bullet is spent.'[4]

Combined South African and Portuguese forces then marched on Mandume and he was killed in action in 1917 in a major battle. Over 100 of his people were also killed or wounded. The South Africans suffered 9 dead and 13 wounded.[5] The head of Chief Mandume was then brought to Windhoek and displayed to show that the resistance had been overcome by the South African forces. It was later buried near the railway station. The South African Administrator later declared:

> The country is now entirely tranquil. Our representatives in Ovamboland will continue to watch the situation closely and do all in their power to induce the able-bodied men of the differernt tribes to go south to engage themselves as labourers on the railways, mines and farms...The supply from the Ukuanyama tribe has been much interrupted of late owing to Mandume's actions, but I am hopeful that it will soon be restored.[6]

There were, however, more major confrontations between South Africa and various Namibian communities before its rule was fully established in the country.

In the south, the Bondelswart community rebelled against South African rule in 1922. One of the leaders of the community was Abraham Morris, who had been active in the 1904–7 war of resistance. Under their treaty with the Germans, the Bondelswarts were compelled to provide labour for public works and private employers (usually farmers), but the wages were very low and sometimes paid only in kind – in food or supplies – and not in cash. Then the South Africans imposed a tax on the people's hunting dogs, to try to force them into further waged employment, and there was considerable resistance which developed into open rebellion. The South Africans' answer was to send in airborne forces and bomb the area. Morris and over 100 other men, women and children were killed, and some 500 wounded or taken prisoner.[7] One South

African soldier involved in the action was prompted to say 'This is not pleasant work ... the people are fighting for the same thing as we fought the English for twenty years ago: freedom. That is all they want.'[8]

The South African regime also clashed with the Rehoboth community in the early 1920s. This was a self-supporting community some 50 miles south of Windhoek, with its own council (Raad) which, through agreement with the Herero Chief Maharero, and later with the German colonial authorities, had managed to retain some degree of autonomy and legislative control over its own affairs. After the mandate over Namibia had been awarded to South Africa, the people of Rehoboth petitioned the League of Nations and the British and South African governments, seeking to retain this independent status, but without success. In 1923 the South African regime persuaded the Raad to agree to its incorporation in the new administrative structures. But the Rehoboth people objected and elected an unofficial body to represent them instead of the Raad. Again, the South African regime responded with force. On 25 April 1925 Rehoboth was surrounded by South African police and soldiers and many people were arrested.[9]

The South African regime also complained that Ukuambi Chief Ipumbu in the north of Namibia showed 'a certain reluctance to submit to the authority of the Commissioner' (Hahn).[10] By the early 1930s this had developed into a situation where South Africa felt its administrative authority was being seriously undermined. As part of a campaign to suppress Ukuambi resistance, South African forces bombed the area, destroying Ipumbu's kraal. Ipumbu himself was deposed by the regime in 1932 and banished to a remote part of the country. The chieftaincy was abolished and a council of headmen was set up in its place.

LABOUR PROTEST

Poverty-level wages, bad working conditions and the contract labour system have been a perpetual focus of protest in Namibia. Attempts to organise Namibian workers into trade union or other organisations have, however, met with severe reprisals from the South African regime.

In the 1920s Luderitz was an important centre for early trade union activity although little is known in detail of their work. In 1924 the South African Administrator stated that 'several unions were in existence' in Luderitz, 'the chief of which were the Universal Negro Improvement Association and a Cape

Coloured institution known as the International and Commercial Workers' Union'.[11]

There is even less information on workers' organisations in the 1930s and 1940s, although it can be seen from Table 1 that there were a number of local strikes during this period, the largest being at the Tsumeb mine in 1948. In the 1950s, the Cape Town based Food and Canning Workers' Union (FCWU) started to organise in Luderitz. The Union President, Frank Marquard, went there in 1949 and was followed in 1952 by the Secretary General, Ray Alexander. The FCWU branch 'probed pay and conditions and pressed for protective industrial legislation'.[12] But the South African regime clamped down on their activities. Police intimidated union members and officials and Alexander was prohibited from trade union involvement under the Suppression of Communism Act. This meant that an important link between Cape Town and Luderitz workers was broken. Nevertheless, there were two big strikes amongst the Luderitz cannery workers in 1952 and 1953. During the latter, three workers were shot dead by the police (see Table 1).

THE FORMATION OF OPC/OPO

The most important development on the labour front during the 1950s, however, was the formation, in 1958, of the Ovamboland People's Congress (OPC). This was formed amongst a group of some 200 Namibian workers based in Cape Town (many were there illegally, having deserted contracts to work on the South African mines). Among the founding members of OPC were Andimba Toivo Ja Toivo (the overall leader), Peter Mueshihange, Solomon Mifima, Andreas Shipanga, Jackson Kashikuka, Jacob Kuhangua and Maxton Joseph Mutongolume. This was an organisation that grew out of the informal support network that existed amongst Namibian workers in Cape Town.

From the start, OPC aimed to improve the conditions of its members and, indeed, other contract workers from Ovamboland. Its members also, however, had close links with the African National Congress of South Africa and the Congress Alliance, and anticipated being part of a broad congress movement in Namibia. Some Namibian students studying in Cape Town were also close to the OPC, in particular Emil Appolus, Jariretundu Kozonguizi and Ottilie Schimming Abrahams.

Table 1 Workers' Strikes in Namibia 1915–59

Year	Place	Known Details
1916		Migrant workers strike for issue of working clothes
1916	Kahn mine	Manager misleads regime in attempt to get police to intimidate workers
1918	Farms	Workers down tools in protests
1923	Luderitz mines	Workers retaliate when one of them is assaulted by a foreman; 17 fined
1925	Conception Bay	Strike threatened; 13 'ringleaders' arrested
1937	Oranjemund mine	Miners strike over use of X-ray examinations for diamonds pilfered by departing migrants
1939	Tsumeb mine	Strike by workers who suspect not receiving pay they are entitled to
1939	Nageib mine	
1948	Tsumeb mine	2,000 strike in protest when a white boy aged 13 shoots dead a worker
1952	Luderitz	Large strike by cannery workers
1953	Walvis Bay	Fish cannery strikes
1953	Luderitz	Fish cannery strikes; 3 workers shot dead by police
1954	Tsumeb	Copper smelter strike over furnace working conditions
1956	Brandberg mine	
1956	Otjisondu mine	
1956	Windhoek	Laundry washerwomen strike
1959	Walvis Bay	Oceana fish cannery; go-slow over an assault of a foreman and attempts to force workers to clean dangerous machinery while in motion; and wages; 12- or 18-hour day; and other working conditions

Source: From Gillian and Suzanne Cronje, The Workers of Namibia (London, International Defence and Aid Fund, 1979), pp. 78–9.

Ja Toivo was educated at St Mary's mission school, an Anglican school in northern Namibia. During the Second World War he served in the South African army. When he was demobilised he went to Cape Town and worked there, studying privately and becoming actively involved in African nationalist politics. Campaigning with the OPC, Ja Toivo wrote to various governments and organisations about the plight of his people and also petitioned the United Nations. His cause was not only the conditions facing the contract workers, but the situation in the country as a whole under the South African regime. His first petition to the United Nations was forwarded in a recorded message hidden in an old copy of Robert Louis Stevenson's *Treasure Island*, and was received in New York on 24 September 1958. He also wrote to the Pope and, as follows, to the British Queen:

> We wish to inform Your Majesty's Government that the Government of South Africa has failed to comply with the provisions embodied in the mandate agreement and also to carry out the international obligations entrusted her by the League of Nations and Your Majesty's Government. We, the people of Ovamboland and the rest of our fellow men in the territory of South West Africa ... hereby appeal to Your Majesty's Government of Great Britain in whose behalf our mandated territory is being administered by the South African Government to revoke the mandate forthwith and to place it under the United Nations Trusteeship System.[13]

His letter to the Queen was returned, however, with a note saying it should be forwarded through her representative, the Governor General of South Africa.

At the end of 1958 Ja Toivo was deported from Cape Town back to Namibia because of his political activities. As he left Cape Town he said:

> I came here ... to study and to gain more experience in political activity. I have made many good friends, particularly among members of the African National Congress. It is now time to return and carry on the struggle in my own country.[14]

On 19 April 1959 the Ovamboland People's Organisation (OPO) was established in Windhoek. Sam Nujoma was elected President; Louis Nelengani, Vice President; Lucas Nepela and Jacob Kuhangua were other key leaders. Nujoma was later described as 'already becoming a legend':

> Once a labourer for the railways, he had been fired for trying to form a union. Now he was blacklisted by the employers and, unable to work, he devoted his time to the Advisory Boards and to community issues. He had

startled everyone by engineering the ousting of his own conservative uncle from the chairmanship of the Ovambo Advisory Board. Though Sam himself was not officially recognized on any of the boards, people all over the location recognized him as one of their real leaders.[15]

OPO campaigned for support amongst the contract workers in factories and mines. Vinnia Ndadi was branch secretary in Walvis Bay, where there was a local membership 'of several thousand' workers.[16] Although OPO primarily focused on the position and welfare of contract workers from the north, it included in its stated objectives the attainment of national independence. It was thus not surprising that in June 1960 OPO changed its name and status to SWAPO – the South West Africa People's Organisation – and began to broaden its membership and appeal.

5 EDUCATIONAL, CULTURAL & CHURCH PROTESTS

Although the Universal Negro Improvement Association (UNIA) was listed by the South African regime as a union, it was essentially a cultural association. The first branch was set up in Luderitz in 1921 by S W Ncwana, a South African from Cape Town. From there it spread to Windhoek, Usakos, Karibib, Okahandja and other urban centres.

The UNIA was founded by the Caribbean leader Marcus Garvey in 1914 after he learned of the conditions under which blacks lived and worked in South America. Its aims were

> To establish a Universal Confraternity among the [black] race; to promote the spirit of race pride and love; to reclaim the fallen; to administer to and assist the needy ... to assist in the development of independent Negro nations and communities ... to establish universities; colleges, academies and schools for the racial education and culture of the people; to work for better conditions among Negroes everywhere.[1]

Garvey's ideas and writings and his slogan 'Africa for the Africans' were welcomed by blacks in southern Africa. In Namibia these ideas came at a crucial time, as South Africa consolidated its control over the country. The fact that Garveyism gained influence in Namibia has been attributed to the broken promises made by the South Africans when they took over Namibia.[2] Its function was similar to that of other cultural associations elsewhere in Africa: they 'made it possible for Africans to recover, within the new urban context, the sense of common purpose which in traditional African society was normally enjoyed through tribal organisation'.[3]

The UNIA in Namibia was vocal in its opposition to South African rule. Fritz Headly, President of the Luderitz branch and a chief stevedore for the Railways and Harbours in Luderitz, summed up their approach as follows: 'This our fatherland must be freed from the white man's rule, for his reign is simply stifling the talents and progressiveness of our people.'[4] Meetings were held at various towns in central and southern

Namibia, with speakers calling for black unity and a black administration in Namibia.

Headly kept in touch with UNIA headquarters in the USA. Indeed, one of the most valuable aspects of the UNIA was the links it established between Namibians and various black political and church groups in South Africa and the USA. Petitions were also sent on Namibia's behalf to the League of Nations, requesting that Namibia 'be turned over to members of the Negro Race for self-government'.[5]

Funds were also raised in Namibia to send to Liberia, where the UNIA was concentrating its back-to-Africa campaign. In fact there was a number of non-Namibians, mostly West Africans, who were members of the UNIA in the country, especially in the Luderitz branch. These were people who had been brought to Namibia by the Germans or who had come as sailors and stayed on in Luderitz to work.

The white community in Namibia felt threatened by UNIA activities. Meetings were monitored by the police and attempts were made to discourage Namibians from having anything to do with UNIA. Support dwindled, however, in the late 1920s. There was no programme of action to bring about the black administration the UNIA demanded. Nevertheless, it did offer a body of thought that promoted a sense of black pride and dignity. It has been stated that

> The Garvey ideology built upon a notion of Negro consciousness had made widespread appeal to the various ethnic groups in central Namibia. Part of its attraction lay in its offer of an alternative identity for the various peoples of that land – an identity which to a large part emerged out of an aspiration for self-determination.[6]

OTJISERANDU

After the battle of Hamakari between the Germans and the Herero people in 1904, many Hereros retreated to the east across the Kalahari desert. They were led by Chief Samuel Maharero and, although there was terrible loss of life during the journey, about one thousand reached safety in Botswana and eventually settled there.

The survival of the overall Herero chief, even though he was in exile, was crucial to the cohesion of the Herero community in Namibia after their defeat by the Germans. In the 1920s there was a growing movement to reaffirm Herero traditions and culture. Some Hereros began to return from exile in Botswana. Others left the Christian churches to which they had been converted, and revived their traditional beliefs and the holy fire, symbol of the community and its connections with past and future. Then in 1923 a new association was formed among the Hereros called *Otjiserandu* – the red band. This came into being at the time of the burial of Chief Samuel Maharero. The body of the chief was brought back to Namibia from Botswana and was buried at the family grave at Okahandja on 26 August 1923, alongside his father Maharero and grandfather Tjamuaha. The ceremony was conducted with full traditional rites.

This funeral became an occasion for the Hereros to honour their dead who had fought against German colonial rule, and to reassert their desire for self-determination. A great number of people attended, including some whites, and even a representative of the South African regime laid a wreath on the grave.

> There were 150 men on horseback, a line of 800 men on foot and a band. This was a symbolic resurrection of the Herero army in the eclectic style which it had adopted before the risings of 1904 to 1907. But, above all, the red scarf, or red band around the arm – the symbols of Chief Maharero's people – were to form the basis of a Herero association, *Otjiserandu*, or Red Band Organisation. It was essentially in order to take care of the arrangements for this occasion that *Otjiserandu* was called into being.[7]

26 August was thereafter commemorated at an annual celebration in Okahandja of Herero tradition and resistance, with a visit to the burial places of the Herero chiefs. Although this was primarily a Herero occasion, increasing numbers of Nama and Damara people also took an active part in the commemoration, appropriately bringing together those communities who had fought the Germans in the 1904–7 war. By historical coincidence, 43 years later, on 26 August 1966, SWAPO embarked on its armed struggle against the South African regime, thus continuing the armed resistance against foreign rule

The *Otjiserandu* was run along military lines, with ranks and uniforms. It became a mutual-aid society as well as a focus for reasserting Herero tradition and for opposition to the South African regime.

PROTESTS OVER EDUCATION

Criticism of the education provided by the missionaries and colonial regimes had been widespread throughout Africa and so it was in Namibia. Educational opportunities were long denied Namibians, and the provision of them, through independent schools, adult literacy classes and, later, scholarships for study abroad, has been a key issue on which Namibian nationalists have campaigned.

When the South Africans took over Namibia from the German colonial authorities, there were only a few schools established for Africans. The teaching was in German and was very elementary, focusing more on German language and culture and on Bible study, than anything else. All the African schools were then run by missionaries. The first state school for Africans set up by the South African regime was opened in Aminuis Reserve in 1935, after a series of protests about inadequate education by the Herero community. Initially it took only 100 pupils. The total number of schools built by the South African regime in Namibia from the beginning of the mandate up to 1940 was only two, both in the central region. Not a single state school was built for Africans in the north between 1920 and 1960. For those Africans in school the standard of education was still very low – up to Standard III only (that is, five years of basic schooling).

By contrast, Tanganyika, which was also a former German colony and then administered by Britain under a League of Nations mandate, was able to send African students with Standard VIII to Makerere College by the 1930s. Even so, educational provision in Tanganyika was low by East African standards.

It has been stated that 'what Africans wanted, at this time and throughout the colonial period, was literary, assimilative education in a European language, for this was seen as the route to high wages, equality and power.'[8] In Namibia, however, the typical white-settler mentality was against this, thinking that

> to educate them is to give them contact with world movements and world thinking which, of course ... inculcates such mischievous and intolerable ideas as democracy, the brotherhood of man, fundamental human freedoms, and the like.[9]

After 1948, moreover, the South African regime developed an even harsher education policy which culminated in the Bantu

27

Education Act of 1953. The clearest statement of the ideology that lay behind this Act came from the then Minister of Native Affairs, Dr Verwoerd, when he said:

> There is no place for ... [the African] in the European community above the level of certain forms of labour.
> ... Education [will be] in Sub-standards A and B, and probably up to Standard II, including reading, writing and arithmetic through mother-tongue instruction, as well as a knowledge of English and Afrikaans, and the cardinal principles of the Christian religion.[10]

English and Afrikaans were to be taught

> in such a way that the Bantu child will be able to find his way in European communities; to follow oral and written instructions and to carry on a simple conversation with Europeans about his work and other subjects of common interest.[11]

The South African system of Bantu Education was extended to cover Namibia following a commission of inquiry headed by Dr Van Zyl.

The Bantu Education system aroused great criticism within South Africa and Namibia. There was also an outcry abroad, particularly in Britain. In Namibia, the opposition came from the African communities, the Anglican and African Methodist Episcopal (AME) churches and the South West Africa Teachers' Association (a group that tried to lobby for better pay and conditions for black teachers, but often without success).

There were some attempts by Namibians to start independent schools to bypass the racist education policies of the South African regime, but they suffered from lack of financial resources. There was always, however, a strong desire for such schools. In 1948, a delegation of Nama leaders, representing the AME church, requested permission to build an independent school or that the regime should supply schools with 'proper subjects up to standard'.[12] Both proposals were rejected, but the AME church went ahead and set up its own schools at various towns in southern Namibia. The schools were not, however, recognised by the South African regime.

Very gradually, more educational facilities were provided by church and state in Namibia. It was not, however, until 1948 that the first black pupil completed secondary schooling and matriculation (Standard X). Even today, the country remains one of the most educationally disadvantaged in Africa.

THE INCIPIENT INTELLIGENTSIA

The educated elite played an important role in nationalist struggles throughout Africa, and in Namibia teachers, students and churchmen were also leading figures in campaigns against the South African regime.

In the 1940s, the African Improvement Society, which had its roots in the earlier UNIA, developed into an important organisation concerned with the provision of educational and cultural opportunities denied to Africans under South African rule. It was based in Windhoek and ran adult education classes for the local African community. Its members were mostly Hereros and included those who had been able to acquire some education and who wanted to share their knowledge with others: men such as Berthold Kangavi Himumuine, Principal of St Barnabas Anglican School where English was taught and where evening literacy classes were run, who won a scholarship to study at Oxford University but was refused a passport by the South African regime; Revds Erwin Tjirimuje and Bartholomew Karuaera, both former students at St Barnabas School and later teachers, and now prominent SWAPO members and leaders of the AME church; Clemens Kapuuo, a teacher who was to become Herero chief in 1970; David Meroro and A.B. Munoko, two local black businessmen. Zed Ngavirue, who taught at St Barnabas and was later Vice-President of the South West Africa National Union (SWANU), was also associated with the AIS in the early 1950s.

In the late 1940s, the Damara community in Windhoek formed a similar body, called Fakkel (meaning 'torch' in Afrikaans). It was essentially a cultural and educational association and was brought into existence because the community felt that the African Improvement Society was dominated by Hereros. Fakkel was active in protesting against the poor educational opportunities for Africans and, in the late 1950s, the forced removal of Damara people from Aukeigas to the planned Damara homeland at Okombahe, and the removal of Africans from Windhoek's Old Location to the new township of Katutura.

The presence of Namibian students in South Africa, where they had to go to study at a secondary or post-secondary level because of the lack of such facilities in Namibia, established useful contacts between nationalists in both countries. Most Namibians went to the Transvaal, although some went to the Cape. While in South Africa they came into contact with the campaigns and protests of the political organisations opposed to the South African regime. Of particular influence were the events in 1952 of the Defiance Campaign of the African National Congress (ANC) and other members of the Congress Alliance, when 8,000 men and women risked imprisonment as they embarked upon a nation-wide peaceful protest against the Pass Laws.

This was the background to the formation of the South West Africa Student Body (SWASB), formed to represent Namibian students in South Africa in the early 1950s. SWASB had close links with nationalist organisations in South Africa such as the ANC, and with people in Namibia. Some of the students who returned home used the experience they had gained of political organisation while in South Africa to form a cultural association, together with their counterparts in Namibia. Formed in 1958, this organisation was known as the South West Africa Progressive Association (SWAPA). The President was Uatja W. Kaukuetu, a young dynamic leader and skilful orator, who had spent several years studying in South Africa.

SWAPA projected itself as a cultural body with a political flavour. Its early projects included organising cultural functions, particularly in Windhoek. It also encouraged pupils and students in the country by offering prizes to those doing the best work. The first recipient was Obed Kaunozondunge, a pupil at the Herero school in the late 1950s. The prize he won was financial support to cover his studies at secondary school level in South Africa. The funds were raised for these prizes by holding dance competitions and through voluntary collections within the community.

SWAPA captured the imagination of the youth and incipient intelligentsia, particularly in Windhoek. It had support from many different Namibian communities. Some members set up the first black newspaper, a weekly entitled *South West News*. However, this did not run for very long as it lacked financial support and the South African regime brought pressure to bear on its founders, who were becoming increasingly involved in wider political campaigns. Nevertheless, its appearance provided Namibians for the first time with a platform for their views. The paper was also used to finance the SWAPA scholarship scheme.

THE INDEPENDENT CHURCH MOVEMENT

The influence of the Christian churches in Namibia spread with the establishment of colonial control. As elsewhere in

Africa, part of the colonisation process was the dominance of the ideas and religion of the new rulers. Large numbers were converted to Christianity. No doubt the churches provided some sense of security and patronage for those whose traditional social structures had been partially destroyed and the Christian message of salvation has always offered hope to those in a seemingly hopeless situation. Moreover, excluded from real participation in the new political institutions of the country, Namibians found in the churches an institution in which they could participate, and which they began to claim as their own.

The practice and teachings of the Christian churches in Southern Africa were, however, distorted by racism and ideas of white supremacy. In South Africa a multitude of sects have sprung up over the years as black people have broken away from the established churches. In Namibia, however, rather than forming a variety of sects, people set up independent churches or simply broke away from the control of the European mission churches. These moves, particularly amongst members of the Lutheran church, were spurred on by dissatisfaction with the particularly close identification of the Lutheran church with the South African regime. Indeed, Dr H Vedder, head of the Rhenish Lutheran Mission in Namibia, accepted an appointment to the South African Senate in 1950.

The first independent African church was the African Methodist Episcopal (AME) church. Originally founded in the USA as the result of a growing group consciousness among black people, its burning desire was that the community should control its own affairs. It established self-help projects to help meet the basic social and educational needs of its members. In the latter part of the nineteenth century this movement spread to Africa and AME churches were established in Ethiopia and South Africa, although it was not until 1947 that it became established in Namibia.

In southern and central Namibia the AME had tremendous appeal. The majority of the people in the south and many in the central part of the country became members and supporters of the church. This included all influential members of the community in the south, including Chief Samuel H Witbooi, who fought the Germans in the war of resistance from 1904 to 1907. The AME is still a thriving church, currently led by Revd B G Karuaera along with Revds H Witbooi and E S Tjirimuje, amongst others. Karuaera and Tjirimuje are Executive Committee members of SWAPO and Witbooi is SWAPO Vice-President. Another dynamic figure who appeared on the scene during the 1940s and 1950s proselytizing for the AME in the central part of Namibia, with his headquarters in Windhoek, was the South African Revd M M Sephula (now in exile in London).

The *Oruuano* church was founded in 1955. Headed originally by Revd Leonard Ruzo, it also led to a big exodus from the Lutheran church, and many Herero members of the AME moved to join the *Oruuano*. The decision to launch it came after lengthy consultations within the community. Its direct approach to issues which affected the lives of its members meant that it was extremely close to the community, in contrast to the white-controlled Lutheran church. The *Oruuano* retained many of the general practices of the parent church in matters of worship, but injected a new and lively element. It has since suffered because of political differences within the Herero community and today only has a small following. It has been stated that the actual break away to form the *Oruuano*

> seems to have been precipitated by the appointment of Dr
> H H Vedder, the spiritual leader of the [Lutheran] church
> to the South African Senate by the late Dr D F Malan in
> 1950. This incident, and Dr Vedder's speeches in the
> Senate in support of apartheid . . . could not be without
> implications on the church.[13]

Protests were also made, however, by those Namibians who remained within the Lutheran church, to try to gain a greater say in the church's affairs. There was gross inequality betwen black and white clergy with the white pastors always in charge. African priests, often quite old but prominent in church structures, used to struggle to maintain themselves and perform their duties as pastors, while their young white counterparts had good housing, transport and all sorts of amenities at their disposal.

Increasing pressure from the black members of the Lutheran church in the 1950s in opposition to racial discrimination within the church structures, finally led to the establishment of the autonomous and locally run Evangelical Lutheran Ovambo-Kavango church (ELOK) in 1956 and the Evangelical Lutheran church (ELK) in 1957. Namibia's first black bishop was Dr Leonard Auala of ELOK, who became head of the church in 1960.

The essence of the upsurge of the new movement in the Christian church in Namibia was caught in the treatment of a biblical text (Matthew 5: 39) traditionally used to suppress anger or resistance:

But what I tell you is this: do not set yourself against the man who wrongs you, If someone slaps you on the right cheek, turn and offer him your left.

In ELOK churches throughout Namibia, pastors went on to say

If we are slapped on the cheek whether by an individual or by the ruling class of our country, in turning the other cheek like Jesus did before Pilate, as Christians we at least have the right to ask, 'Why are you slapping me?'[14]

Thus began a process whereby the church increasingly questioned and challenged the South African regime in Namibia.

6 PETITIONS TO THE UNITED NATIONS

In 1945–6 the League of Nations was wound up and its place taken by the new United Nations Organization. South Africa took this opportunity to try to incorporate Namibia fully into the Union. The UN immediately established a trusteeship system, with independence as its specific goal, for the former mandated territories. All the other former German colonies in Africa – the Cameroons, Togoland, Tanganyika and Ruanda Urundi – were put under the trusteeship system in 1946. But South Africa did not consider that the UN carried on the League's supervisory role over the mandated territories. It pleaded that Namibia's proximity to South Africa made it a special case, and requested time to consult the people of Namibia on the country's future. A campaign against incorporation into South Africa was then launched in Namibia, and drew different Namibian communities together in opposition to the South African regime.

From December 1945 to April 1946 the South African regime held what it termed 'consultations' with Namibian leaders supposedly to ascertain their views on the planned incorporation. General Smuts himself even visited Namibia at this time. Traditional leaders and headmen were called to meetings where they were addressed by South African officials and told how the South African regime had rescued Namibians from the 'chaos' of German rule, given them land (!), education and economic assistance.[1] They were asked whether they wanted any other nation to rule them and given the following document to sign:

> We the undersigned ... Chiefs, Headmen or Board Members of the people of the _____ tribe, who live in the _____ Reserve in this Mandated Territory of South West Africa, acting with full authority of the people of the tribe of the Reserve, wish to say that we have heard that the people of the world are talking about the administration of countries such as ours, and that the Administration of those countries may be changed.
>
> We and our people wish the following matters to be made known to the peoples of the world:

34

1. that our people have been happy and have prospered under the Rule of the Government of the Union of South Africa and that we should like that Government to continue to rule us;
2. that we do not wish any other Government or people to rule us; and
3. that we would like our country to become part of the Union of South Africa.[2]

The results claimed by the South African regime were that the whites, through their Legislative Assembly, had voted for incorporation, and that of the blacks, 208,850 were in favour, 33,520 were against, and 56,870 had not been consulted. They hoped to convince the United Nations with these figures, but the reality of this so-called vote was that Namibian leaders who had opposed incorporation had been overruled, and the views of those who supported incorporation were 'attributed to all members of their tribes, including new-born babies'.[3] The chiefs were also subject to reprisals by the South African regime if they did not do as they were told.

Leaders from all the various Namibian communities claimed that they had not been asked about incorporation or that their opinions had not been listened to.[4] A missionary of nine years' experience working in Namibia reported of this so-called referendum: 'It was an absolute farce. That is what even one of the native Commissioners said about it.'[5]

The Herero Chief Hosea Komombumbi Kutako (fondly referred to as 'Katjikururume') was the leading figure in the petitioning of the United Nations against incorporation which then began. He requested that a UN Commission be allowed to visit Namibia to conduct the referendum, but this was refused by the South African regime. Then he asked for four of his spokesmen to be allowed to go to the UN, but this was also turned down. The South African regime would not give such black leaders passports to leave Namibia and lobby the world body. Kutako therefore sent telegrams to the UN to try to sway the General Assembly. Petitions against the incorporation of Namibia into South Africa were also sent to the UN by the chiefs in Botswana, the All-African Convention of South Africa (which represented a wide range of political, social, religious and traditional black groups), Dr A B Xuma, President-General of the ANC of South Africa, and from many other sources.[6]

At the UN itself the campaign against incorporation was led by the Indian delegation, whose representative, Sir Maharaj Singh, had represented India as Agent-General in South Africa.

Britain spoke in favour of incorporation but abstained in the vote. The USA finally came out against incorporation, and on 14 December 1946 the UN General Assembly rejected South Africa's request to incorporate Namibia. The voting was 37 votes to 0, with 9 abstentions.

Although incorporation had been avoided the General Assembly also declared that it felt that Namibians

> Have not yet . . . reached a stage of political development enabling them to express a considered opinion which the Assembly could recognise on such an important question as incorporation.[7]

This only added to the desire of those Namibians active in the campaign against incorporation to have a voice at the UN, so that they could properly express their discontent with South African rule. Through the initiatives of Herero Chiefs Hosea Kutako (based in Namibia) and Frederick Maharero (the overall chief, based in exile in Botswana), and with the assistance of Ngwato Chief Tshekedi Khama, a remarkable campaign had already been launched. A British clergyman, Revd Michael Scott, became the intermediary and representative of the Herero and other Namibian communities and presented the UN with petitions from them that opposed incorporation, but also that went beyond this issue and challenged the record of South African rule in Namibia.

THE BOTSWANA CONNECTION

The Herero community in Botswana was formed by people leaving Namibia to escape German and South African rule. The largest group arrived during the 1904–7 war of resistance against the Germans, after the battle of Hamakari. This group included the Herero Chief Samuel Maharero. He eventually settled in Serowe in eastern Botswana. He maintained close contact, however, with the Herero community in Namibia through Chief Hosea Kutako and his Chief's Council. Kutako himself had fought in the 1904 war against the Germans and had escorted Samuel Maharero across the border into Botswana. He pledged to the chief that he would safeguard and lead those Hereros who remained in Namibia, and he returned to Namibia to do this. Samuel Maharero's son and successor, Frederick Maharero, visited Namibia in 1923 to accompany the body of his father for burial. He used this occasion to confirm Kutako's position as head of the Herero community in Namibia.

When, therefore, the South African regime initiated its plans to incorporate Namibia, there was much correspondence between Kutako and his spokesmen and their compatriots in Botswana. These letters urged the Herero community in Botswana to act and, specifically, to petition Britain on Namibia's behalf. One such letter, from one of Kutako's lieutenants in the Chief's Council, went as follows:

> We are being asked that our land be joined to the Union, but we refused, stating that our land will not be joined to the Union at all, but rather that it should remain ours only, together with those with whom we have been associating in the past. That is what we said ... the Hereros, the Namas, the Ovambos and the Berg Damaras have all refused ... We have been informed that on 3rd September there will be a meeting again, that we would be stopped from going to that meeting, and that they will have their own man to speak for them while we will be stopped. This is all. *The matter now rests with you. You who enjoy freedom are the people who should come here to us.*[8]

Frederick Maharero's first step was to draw in African leaders in Botswana. They were already concerned that if Namibia were incorporated into South Africa, attempts would be made to incorporate Botswana and the other British High Commission territories of Swaziland and Lesotho. In April 1946, therefore, the Botswana chiefs sent a memorandum to the British government opposing the incorporation of Namibia into South Africa. The Ngwato Chief Tshekedi Khama was particularly active in this campaign, and tried to visit London to lobby the British government personally, but he was not allowed to do so. Instead, he introduced Revd Michael Scott to the Namibian issue.

THE ROLE OF MICHAEL SCOTT

Scott was an Anglican priest working in South Africa who had become very involved in protests against the system of racial discrimination and spent some months in jail for his part in a civil disobedience campagin. In late 1946 he met Frederick Maharero, who invited him to visit Namibia as his emissary and gather information on the situation there and the progress of South Africa's incorporation plans. When he arrived in Windhoek, Scott made contact with Chief Kutako's principal secretary and interpreter, Berthold Himumuine, and was taken to meet Namibian leaders who had taken part in the campaign against incorporation, including Kutako himself.

After extensive talks and after taking statements from various Namibian leaders, Scott was convinced that 'great injustices had been and were going to be committed.'[9] He returned to Botswana to report to Frederick Maharero and together they drew up a detailed petition to go to the United Nations. It outlined the history of the Hereros from the time of the German colonial regime; the war of extermination, the loss of their lands, and conditions under South African rule. It then asked for the return of Herero lands by South Africa, the return of the Paramount Chief Frederick Maharero and the reunification of the Herero community in one area within Namibia. It argued that Namibia should not remain under South Africa as a mandated territory but be placed under UN trusteeship or, failing that, become a British Protectorate or, failing that, be placed under the protection of the USA.[10]

Then Scott returned to Namibia, taking the draft petition with him for Chief Kutako and his colleagues to examine and approve. The final preparation and ceremony for the signature of these historic documents coincided with the annual Herero commemoration of Otjiserandu, held around 26 August. At the signing Chief Kutako prayed for the deliverance of the Namibian people:

> You are the Great God of all the Earth and the Heavens. We are so insignificant. In us there are many defects. But the Power is yours to make and to do what we cannot do. You know all about us. For coming down to earth you were despised, and mocked, and brutally treated because of those same defects in the men of those days. And for those men you prayed because they did not understand what they were doing, and that you came only for what was right. Give us the courage to struggle in that way for what is right.
>
> O Lord, help us who roam about. Help us who have been placed in Africa and have no dwelling place of our own. Give us back a dwelling place. O God, all power is yours in Heaven and Earth. Amen.[11]

The South African regime tried to prevent Scott from taking the petition to the UN, and started a campaign to try to discredit Scott, labelling him a crank and follower of left-wing causes. But his involvement gave the Namibian people a voice at the UN. It 'transformed the South West African issue from a tedious, legal wrangle with a minor goverment into a crusade to save a people'.[12] For Scott himself, the Hereros had become 'symbolical of all the landless and dispossessed people in the world'.[13]

From 1947 on, Scott was locked in battle at the UN with South Africa. He returned to Namibia once more and again encountered problems trying to fly out, having to travel by road to the Congo before he was able to get a plane to Europe. South Africa banned him from visiting Namibia in 1948 and for a while Mary Benson went on his behalf to contact Namibian leaders until she too was refused entry.

Throughout the 1950s Chief Kutako continued to compile information on conditions in Namibia and use it to petition the UN. He has been described as the 'chief inspirer and leader of the post-war resistance movement which became the main source of modern nationalism'.[14] The Chief's Council, which Kutako led, increasingly took in traditional leaders from other communities, such as Nama Chief Samuel Witbooi, leading personalities from the Damara and Ovambo communities, including the Anglican priest Revd T. Hamutumbangela, as well as Herero headmen and advisers. Kutako applied for permission to visit the north of the country to make contact with traditional leaders there, but this was refused him by the South African regime. In any case, most of the chiefs in the north were directly employed by, and therefore under obligation to, the South African authorities. In particular, Ondonga Chief Johannes Kambonde co-operated with the South African regime and helped to suppress opposition to it. In 1956 Andimba Ja Toivo wrote to Mburumba Kerina urging him to use his influence on Kambonde to 'inform him the present position of S.W.A.'. He went on: 'I think it would also be a good thing if you could ask him to get in touch with Chief Hosea Kutako and other chiefs.'[15] However, this did not come about.

The first Namibian to give evidence at the UN was Mburumba Kerina, in 1957, when he was studying at Lincoln University. Then in 1959 the Herero Chief's Council sent Jariretundu Kozonguizi to the UN with the specific task of petitioning on Namibia's behalf. That same year Hans Beukes, who had a scholarship to study in Oslo but no passport, was smuggled out of Namibia by three young Americans and he also later appeared at the UN.[16]

By the end of the 1950s and early 1960s, increasing numbers of Namibians managed to get to the UN to testify on conditions in the country. Most had left their country because of South African repression of political activity. These included Jacob Kuhangua, Marcus Kooper, Sam Nujoma and Louis Nelengani (President and Vice-President of SWAPO respectively), and Ismail Fortune. Oliver Tambo, then Deputy President-General of the ANC of South Africa, and Eduardo Mondlane, President of FRELIMO, also petitioned the UN on Namibia's behalf. 'In 1946 there had been a solitary petition in the form of a cable . . . in 1960, 120 petitions were directed at the United Nations Fourth Committee. Political organization was stirring in South West Africa.'[17]

7 THE EMERGENCE
OF NATIONALIST ORGANISATIONS

1958–60 were the years during which the various strands of Namibian opposition to South African rule came together and developed into a self-consciously nationalist movement. These were:

1 The incipient intelligentsia and bodies such as the South West Africa Student Body (SWASB) and the South West Africa Progressive Association (SWAPA).

2 The contract workers through the Ovamboland People's Congress (OPC) set up in Cape Town in 1958 and which later developed into the Ovamboland People's Organisation (OPO) in 1959.

3 The Herero Chief's Council, whose role was the co-ordinating and leading of petitions to the UN.

In 1958 opposition to South African rule was led by Chief Kutako and the Herero Chief's Council, and a small group of active nationalists. Mburumba Kerina, Jariretundu Kozonguizi and Zedekia Ngavirue had been active in SWASB but this organisation had largely ceased to function and SWAPA, led by Uatja Kaukuetu and others, had taken its place. Kerina was by this time in the USA studying and petitioning the UN. Kozonguizi had signed Kerina's credentials to petition the UN on SWASB's behalf. He himself was in South Africa, studying at Fort Hare University, where he was on the executive of the student branch of the ANC of South Africa. Andimba Ja Toivo was working in Cape Town. He was closely involved in African nationalist politics there and had connections with the ANC, and the South African Communist and Liberal Parties. He was corresponding with Kerina and Chief Kutako. Peter Mueshihange and the group mentioned above (see chapter 4) were politically active in Cape Town: amongst this group OPC was formed.

Kozonguizi played an important role at this time, linking these various groups and strands of resistance. He was a member of the Herero Chief's Council and tried to bridge the gap between the Council and elders and the younger generation in the student bodies who were 'growing impatient of debating-society politics, and anxious to replace tribal divisions with an aggressive and popular nationalism'.[1] Ja Toivo had also met Kozonguizi in Cape Town.

It was amongst these Namibian activists that the idea of a national body dedicated to the attainment of Namibian independence was born. On the eve of Ja Toivo's deportation from Cape Town to Namibia in 1958, Kozonguizi

addressed the Ovambos organized around Toivo on plans to integrate the emergent Ovamboland People's Organisation into a South West African national congress, based on regional congresses in Namaland (the south), Damaraland (the central area), and Ovamboland.[2]

Kozonguizi travelled to Namibia with Ja Toivo and they stopped at Keetmanshoop to discuss the idea with a new association called the Society for the Advancement of the African People in South West Africa (SAAPSWA), led by Philip Musikira. In Windhoek they spoke to Chief Kutako and Clemens Kapuuo, a teacher and leading member of the Herero community. 'It was agreed that Kozonguizi would organise from the capital, and Toivo from Ovamboland.'[3]

In Ovamboland, Ja Toivo was placed under house arrest under the supervision of Chief Kambonde, but after the chief's death he was able to move freely within Ovamboland. He or one of his lieutenants would go to meetings organised by officials of the South African regime and would attack government policy and demand UN intervention. Kozonguizi, however, did not stay long in Windhoek. He was sent to New York in 1959 by the Herero Chief's Council to reinforce the efforts of Michael Scott petitioning the UN.

THE FORMATION OF SWANU

A constitutional committee chaired by Zedekia Ngavirue was set up in 1959 by the Herero Chief's Council to discuss the idea of a national political organisation. SWAPA activists and members of the Chief's Council were on the committee. The name of the proposed new organisation – the South West Africa National Union (SWANU) – was proposed by Clemens Kapuuo.

The intention of the Chief's Council was 'to graft the modern machinery of a mass organisation upon the traditional system of authority', but the SWAPA activists aimed at 'creating a new movement with new symbols, transcending traditional loyalties'.[4]

When SWANU was officially launched in August 1959, the SWAPA activists took the major leadership posts, with Uatja Kaukuetu as President. This led to a move by the Chief's Council for new elections to broaden the SWANU Executive Committee. In September 1959 a public meeting was held for this purpose. A few hundred people attended, including representatives of the various communities in Windhoek, and Sam Nujoma of OPO. Kozonguizi was the presidential candidate supported by the Chief's Council and he was duly elected in his absence. Kaukuetu became Vice-President; Uaseta Mbuha, Organising Secretary; Nathaniel Mbaeva, Publicity Secretary; Louis Nelengani, Emil Appolus, Sam Nujoma and Damara Chief Kariseb were Executive Committee members.

SWANU was 'conceived as an umbrella organisation which would bring together the different elements of anti-colonial resistance into a single nationalist organisation'.[5] The representation of OPO and various community leaders on the SWANU Executive Committee was, therefore, in line with this aim. SWANU was trying to be a broad-based organisation and regarded OPO's participation as the first step towards a genuine national body. OPO, as a regional organisation representing the particular interests of contract workers, was keen to ally itself with other groups opposed to the South African regime.

SWANU's motto was 'Fortune becometh the daring'. Its stated aims and objectives were:

(a) To unite and rally the people of South West Africa into one National Front.

(b) To fight relentlessly for the implementation and maintenance of the right of self-determination for the people of South West Africa.

(c) To promote the Educational, Cultural and Economic advancement of the People of South West Africa.

(d) To work with allied movements in Africa for the propagation and promotion of the concept of Pan-Africanism and unity amongst the peoples of Africa.

(e) To work with allied movements in Africa, Asia and other Continents with a view to the abolition of imperialism, tribalism, racialism and all forms of oppression, and economic exploitation amongst the People of the world.[6]

Despite the intervention of the Herero Chief's Council to secure a SWANU leadership more favourable to the Council, friction soon developed between the two bodies. After becoming SWANU President, Kozonguizi began to distance himself from what he increasingly regarded as the tribal politics of the

43

Council. It was, in turn, protective of its standing as a body that had led anti-South African protest for many years. The Council felt threatened by the young incoming nationalist leaders and wanted to retain its own power base and some continuity. Its members certainly did not wish to see relatively young and inexperienced people take over. The fact that most of SWANU's leaders were Hereros added to the Council's feelings that its authority was being undermined.

Then in early 1960 a serious controversy arose within the Herero community over who should succeed Chief Kutako, who was then already 90. Clemens Kapuuo was the leading candidate but he was widely criticised by some of his colleagues on the Council and by a section of the SWANU leadership.[7] He was, however, the choice of the Chief, and in March 1960 he was elected as Kutako's deputy, with the unwritten assumption that he would succeed Kutako. The dispute led to the withdrawal the next month (April) of several of Chief Kutako's councillors from SWANU's Executive Committee. Kutako called for Kozonguizi's resignation and for all Hereros to leave SWANU, although this did not happen.

THE FORMATION OF SWAPO

From New York, Kerina corresponded throughout 1959 and into early 1960 with Kapuuo, Nujoma and Ja Toivo, urging united action against the South African regime. When he was joined at the UN by Kozonguizi, who was mandated by the Chief's Council and also elected President of SWANU, it seems that Kerina became anxious to strengthen his own power base and position. One particular letter of his to Ja Toivo, dated 17 November 1959, stated:

I have been urging Mr Nujoma to change the name of the Ovamboland Peoples Organisation into the South West African National Congress. This will give the organisation a national character which can be of great use to our position here.[8]

By early 1960, according to one source, OPO was 'about to be converted into a rival to SWANU'.[9] It still co-operated with SWANU but 'its role in the new national movement was not defined'.[10] Indeed, Solomon Mifima, a founder member of SWAPO, maintains that 'from the beginning there was confusion' about how SWANU and OPO related to each other.[11]

With the withdrawal of Chief Kutako's support from SWANU in April 1960 the way was open for the emergence of a new national body. It has been claimed that OPO leaders were influenced in their course of action by the Chief's Council's move against SWANU,[12] and Kozonguizi approached Nujoma at a meeting in Monrovia in June 1960 to talk about unity. The two leaders agreed on a merger between SWANU and OPO, and possibly a new name as well. The merger was, however, opposed by Kerina in New York and the Chief's Council in Windhoek, and never took effect. Almost immediately thereafter OPO leaders went ahead with plans to transform the organisation into a broader movement and reconstituted it as the South West Africa People's Organisation (SWAPO). Sam Nujoma retained the post of President.

Even today SWAPO celebrates 19 April as its birthdate, but it was OPO that was formed on 19 April, and reconstituted as SWAPO in June 1960. It was not, however, until September 1960 that SWAPO's name was heard at a major international forum. This was when Chief Kutako, Chief Samuel Witbooi and SWAPO jointly petitioned the UN. In November 1960 SWAPO leaders Sam Nujoma (President), Mburumba Kerina (Chairman), Ismail Fortune (Secretary General) and Jacob Kuhangua (Assistant Secretary General) appeared before the UN Fourth Committee on behalf of SWAPO.

SWAPO's motto was 'Work in Solidarity for Justice and Freedom'. Its aims and objectives were:

(a) ... to establish a free, democratic Government in South West Africa founded upon the will and participation of all the people of our country and co-operate to the fullest extent with all our African brothers and sisters to rid our continent of all forms of foreign domination and to rebuild it according to the desires of the African peoples.

(b) To work for the unification of all the people of South West Africa into a cohesive representative, National Political organization, irrespective of their race, ethnic origin, religion or creed.

(c) To work for the achievement of a complete independence for South West Africa and the removal of all forms of oppression such as Apartheid laws, Contract system, Bantu Education, and the introduction of universal adult Suffrage and direct democratic representation of all inhabitants of South West Africa in all organs of the government.

(d) To work for a speedy reconstruction of a better South West Africa in which the people and their Chiefs shall have the right to live and govern themselves as free people.

(e) Reconstruction of the economy, educational and social foundations which will support and maintain the real African independence which our people desire for themselves.

(f) Maintenance of contact, exchange of views and information and co-operation with organisations and individuals dedicated with us to the total emancipation and reconstruction of our continent.[13]

In September 1960 SWAPO discarded its previous policy of favouring UN trusteeship for Namibia, leading to independence, and supported a specially constituted UN authority to 'facilitate the transfer of sovereignty from [the] South African administration to a democratically established African government'.[14]

The first programme SWAPO published called for 'national independence now under an African Government and not later than 1963'. It advocated a 'transitional period' when a UN Commission made up of independent African states would act 'in an advisory capacity' to the new government in Namibia. Economic aims included the public ownership of the railways, mining, electrical and fishing industries, the development of African-owned industry and foreign capital if invested in industries controlled by Namibians. Forced and contract labour were to be abolished. Education was to be free, compulsory and publicly operated. 'All existing lands with foreign title deed and ownership' were to be 'placed under the Government in conformity with African communal ownership principles'.[15]

Early SWAPO letterheads listed branches in Windhoek, Gobabis, Kaokoveld, Okahandja, Oranjemund, Otjiwarongo, Ovamboland, Luderitz, Swakopmund, Tsumeb and Usakos. The 22 national committee members included Nujoma, Kerina, Fortune, Kuhangua, Nathaniel Mahuilili (Acting President after Nujoma left the country in early 1960), Louis Nelengani (Vice-President), Andimba Ja Toivo (Regional Organiser, Ovamboland), Vinnia Ndadi (Regional Chairman, Tsumeb), Eliaser Tuhadeleni Kahumba, J Shoombe, Hans Beukes, V Eixab, and Revd T Hamutumbangela. The majority of these officials were drawn from the previous OPO leadership.

8 EARLY NATIONALIST ACTIVITY & SOUTH AFRICA'S RESPONSES

One of the principal methods adopted by nationalist movements throughout Africa was that of civil disobedience or passive resistance. In South Africa in the 1950s the ANC and other like-minded organisations launched the Defiance Campaign, as well as mass stay-at-homes, demonstrations, boycotts of buses, burning of passes, etc. The ANC Freedom Charter was adopted in 1955, calling for equal rights for all South Africans, redistribution of the country's wealth on an equitable basis and individual civil rights protected by law.

Many of the Namibian students, teachers and workers who formed OPO and SWANU were in South Africa during this time, and the effect of these political developments on Namibian nationalist organisations should not be overlooked. But it was not until 1958-9 that a similar campaign of civil disobedience was launched in Namibia – over the forced removal of people from their existing settlements to the reserves or to newly built black townships.

In 1958 a 400-strong Damara community at Aukeigas, a good farming area, were forcibly removed by the South African regime to the barren Okombahe reserve (see Map 7). In the journey thousands of the people's cattle died. Damara leader Fritz Gariseb saw it as the end of his community. The area they left in Aukeigas was partly bought by white farmers and partly turned into a game reserve, proving that under the South African regime 'even the animals have more state protection than human souls.'[1]

The Nama community at Hoachanas was also threatened with removal. People there described the new area allocated to them, near Tses, as 'just good for a graveyard',[2] and refused to go. Their leader, Revd Marcus Kooper, mounted a campaign against the removal. Then in January 1959 South African police forced him and a small group of his people into lorries and took them to Tses. The community was split apart. But Kooper raised the matter at the United Nations and the ensuing international opposition prevented South Africa from completing the removals.

The biggest campaign was, however, launched to oppose the removal of people from the Old Location in Windhoek to a new township that came to be known as 'Katutura', meaning 'we have no dwelling place'. This was the fifth move of Africans living in Windhoek, enforced by the German and South African regimes. Various committees were formed in the Old Location in opposition to this move, and it has been suggested that the need to present a united front against the regime on this issue may have been a factor in the formation of SWANU.[3]

The Old Location was a shanty town with no proper facilities, but Namibian families had lived there for generations and had freehold rights to the land and there was a strong community spirit there. The regime claimed that the accommodation in Katutura was better, but it was some five miles outside Windhoek. Rents and bus fares would be higher. Worst of all, however, the inhabitants were to be divided into different sections, based on their ethnic group. Coloured (mixed race) Namibians were to be moved to another township altogether – Khomasdal – where they were to have better houses than those for Africans in Katutura. The sick, old and unemployed from the Old Location were to be moved to the reserves.

Opposition to the removals built up through 1959, uniting OPO, SWANU, the Herero Chief's Council and other community groupings. Public meetings were organised but all objections were ignored by the regime. Even the black members of the Advisory Board set up by the South African regime to advise the white municipal authorities on matters concerning the Old Location, were against the move to Katutura.

On 4 December hundreds of Namibian women marched on the buildings of the municipal administration to protest against the move. The next day (5 December), people gathered to organise a boycott of municipal services including the buses and beer hall. This was immediately effective. Then on 10 December some pickets outside the beer hall were arrested and a crowd gathered in protest outside the municipal buildings. Police reinforcements arrived with arms and ammunition and fired on the crowd. Eleven people were killed immediately; two more died the next day. 54 more were injured. Many women had been actively involved in the boycott and demonstrations and one, Anna Kakurukaze Mungunda, was one of those who died. She was shot after setting fire to the car belonging to the white superintendent of the Old Location.

The Windhoek Shootings were raised at the United Nations by the UN Committee on South West Africa, who called on the South African regime to 'stop the deplorable use of force'.[4] But the South African regime blamed Namibian petitioners to the UN for organising opposition to the removals in an attempt to get the UN to intervene in Namibia.[5]

Whites in Namibia responded by rushing to arm themselves, buying up guns and ammunition. SWANU and OPO leaders were ordered out of Windhoek within 72 hours. Fourteen Africans were arrested on charges of public violence and tried in 1961, in Namibia's first big 'political' trial, although they were eventually acquitted. The situation after the shootings was described by the black newspaper *South West News* as 'a reign of terror characterized by arrests, pass refusals, dismissals from jobs, prohibition and deportation orders'.[6] Chief Kutako described it as 'critical and it could lead to war'. He spoke of a 'strong police and military build-up in the territory along its boundaries between Bechuanaland and South West Africa and between Angola and South West Africa'.[7] Some people began to move to Katutura out of fear of further violence from the regime. The homes of African nationalists were raided and documents and letters removed. Many leading nationalists felt compelled to leave the country for fear of their safety, including Sam Nujoma. Most headed for Dar es Salaam, where SWANU and SWAPO established offices.

UNITY AND CONFLICT

Both SWANU and SWAPO campaigned politically within Namibia for independence, although interestingly the SWANU constitution only spoke of 'self-determination'. Both also petitioned the UN although SWANU put less stress on the role of the UN and accused SWAPO of making 'a career out of petitioning'.[8]

The structures of the two organisations were at first very similar, but their support-base and orientation were different. SWANU's founders were the educated elite who wanted new forms of political organisation and to 'give the liberation struggle in SWA a militant and progressive basis'.[9] However, the conflict that developed between them and the Herero Chief's Council , which was in 1960 still the focus of anti-South African activity, partly inhibited SWANU's growth. Moreover, SWANU made no real attempts to win support from communities other than the Hereros or from other social groups. It saw itself as an umbrella organisation and expected other groups to work with it, rather than campaigning for support.

SWAPO membership was, at first, largely made up of contract workers who were former OPO members, However it soon began to include a number of people from other communities and social groups. Co-operation also grew between SWAPO and the Herero Chief's Council in the early 1960s. This brought SWAPO new members from the Herero community, many of them young secondary school students. Kerina was very close to Clemens Kapuuo and Revd B G Karuaera, both leading members of the Council. Kapuuo was then also close to Nujoma and SWANU complained of Kapuuo and Kerina trying to undermine it.

SWANU, already claiming to be the national body, found it difficult to accept the emergence of SWAPO. Organisational conflict was also made worse by competition at the leadership level, especially between Kozonguizi and Kerina:

[They] were the first two Namibian petitioners at the United Nations ... [they] were also the first college-educated Namibians on the nationalist political scene at that time. Kerina and Kozonguizi, therefore, saw themselves as the sole competitors for national leadership, and their rivalry was sharpened by the illusion of an imminent independence to be achieved under the auspices of the United Nations.[10]

There were numerous attempts at uniting the two organisations in some way, but none of them was really successful. At a conference in Accra in June 1962 Kozonguizi and Nujoma signed an agreement proposing that SWANU and SWAPO formally co-operate in their work, but nothing came of it. Kerina pushed so hard for uniting the two organisations that he fell out with the rest of the SWAPO leadership and left the organisation in 1962 (he claimed he had resigned but SWAPO stated that he had been expelled).[11]

In October 1963 a united front, the South West Africa National Liberation Front (SWANLIF) was formed on the joint initiative of SWANU and SWAPO executive committees in Windhoek. It aimed

(a) To solicit aid for the Liberation Movement in South West Africa.
(b) To inform the world at large about South West Africa.
(c) To represent the people of South West Africa in the Councils of the world.
(d) To acquaint the people of South West Africa of the developments in the world at large.[12]

Apart from SWANU and SWAPO it included the South West Africa United National Independence Organisation

(SWAUNIO), based in the south of Namibia, the Burgher Association of Rehoboth, the Rehoboth Council, and the Volks-Organisasie van Suidwes-Afrika (VOSWA), mainly made up of Coloureds living in central Namibia. SWANLIF did not, however, achieve much. The Herero Chief's Council did not join it. Moreover, the SWAPO leadership abroad were not enthusiastic. SWAPO Vice-President Louis Nelengani claimed in 1964 that 'the whole idea of the front is unacceptable ... What do we want in this so-called front which we cannot get in SWAPO?'[13]

In 1963 a regional anti-South African group, the Caprivi African National Union (CANU) was established. Its stated policy was 'national independence now' but its constitution spoke only of 'liberation' of the Caprivi Strip.[14] Bredan Kangongola Simbwaye was President and Mishake Muyongo Vice-President. In November 1964 CANU and SWAPO came together in what was supposed to be a merger, declaring that the two bodies ' cease to exist as separate organisations, we further resolve that CANU and SWAPO merge and unite [as] one Organisation.'[15] Simbwaye became SWAPO Vice-President and Mishake Muyongo the SWAPO Representative in Zambia. Unfortunately, however, there was a difference of opinion as to how the merger would operate. CANU believed that it existed in its own right and was working in alliance with SWAPO, but in practice CANU members were absorbed into SWAPO. The issue was never resolved. It caused trouble in the mid-1960s and later, in 1980, Muyongo (by then Acting Vice-President of SWAPO) was expelled from the organisation for having revived CANU as a splinter group. Simbwaye was detained by the South African authorities in 1964. His current whereabouts remain unknown. There have, however, been reports that he was killed by the South Africans in the late 1970s.

Other small organisations which opposed the South African regime in Namibia in the mid-1960s were: (1) South West Africa Democratic Union (SWADU) – a Damara group; (2) Damara Tribal Executive Committee – established to oppose the pro-South African Damara Chief Goraseb. One of its leading members, Adolf Gariseb, became Chairman of SWAPO in 1962; (3) Namib Convention Independence Party (NACIP) and United Namib Independence People's Party (UNIPP) – both founded by Mburumba Kerina seeking to establish some kind of political base within the country although he was still abroad.

In 1964 the Herero Chief's Council also formed its own political party – the National Unity Democratic Organisation

(NUDO). Chief Hosea Kutako, Clemens Kapuuo and Mburumba Kerina were elected as its leaders. There was very little difference between the activities of NUDO and the Chief's Council, except that NUDO was probably formed as an attempt by the Council to give itself a new, overtly political image to enable it to compete with SWANU and SWAPO. The Council's split with Kozonguizi was, by this time, complete. Relations with SWAPO were still good but as SWAPO grew in strength and membership it increasingly acted on its own rather than in close co-operation with other groups.

No serious attempt was made to win support for NUDO from communities other than the Hereros and the Chief's Council still continued to function. Despite the rivalry between the various nationalist groupings at this time, Chief Kutako was still seen by many African nationalists, young and old, as being above the conflict. He was a respected figure whose leadership qualities and dedication to Namibia's freedom were unquestioned.

OAU SUPPORT

The attainment by many African countries of their independence in the early 1960s had an impact on the nationalist movement in Namibia. Despite the country's isolation, developments in the rest of the continent and, in particular, the independence of Ghana and the crisis in the Congo were followed closely. Namibian nationalists who left the country to campaign abroad for independence co-operated with nationalists from other African countries and the Organisation of African Unity (OAU) which was set up in May 1963.

The OAU set up a Co-ordination Committee for the Liberation of Africa in Dar es Salaam, with a Special Liberation Fund, made up of obligatory contributions from each member state. The committee was intended to co-ordinate assistance to the nationalist movements from countries not yet independent. The question of unity was seen as paramount, however, and where there was more than one organisation from a given country, the committee tried to encourage the formation of a united front or a unified party. Support was offered to those organisations which produced effective and convincing programmes of action and who were seen to have the support of the people they claimed to represent.

Initially, both SWANU and SWAPO were recognised by the OAU, but by mid-1965 SWAPO had secured recognition as the

only nationalist organisation through which the OAU would
support the people of Namibia. Emil Appolus has recounted
why:

> The first budget of the Liberation Committee contained
> the princely sum of £20,000 . . . as 'material and financial
> assistance' to South West Africa, to be divided equally
> among the two political parties then in existence:
> SWANU and SWAPO. The proviso, however, was that the
> liberation movements present a plan of armed struggle
> before the money could be released. We in SWAPO
> immediately declared that we were ready to pick up guns
> to fight what we termed the illegal occupation of our
> country by South Africa. SWANU, on the other hand, said
> they were not prepared for a military confrontation . . .
> this automatically cut off their future prospects of getting
> any financial assistance from any government in Africa.[16]

SWANU had originally been better established in the
international community than SWAPO. It was the first national
body in Namibia and its leadership abroad were an impressive
team with considerable organisational experience. But they
were scattered and largely based in Europe as students,
whereas SWAPO leaders abroad were concentrated in Dar es
Salaam and other African centres and were full-time political
activists. Moreover SWANU leaders seem to have been curiou-
sly passive about the whole process of recognition from the
OAU, as if they took their recognition for granted, and were
then resigned to the inevitability of its being refused.

At a conference in Sweden in May 1965 SWANU elected an
External Council to co-ordinate its work abroad. An overall
strategy for the organisation was drawn up, and the President,
Jariretundu Kozonguizi, planned to return to Namibia in June
1966 to inform the SWANU executive there of these decisions.
However, Kozonguizi came into conflict with other SWANU
leaders over this trip. He accused the SWANU External Council
of sabotaging his work and promptly resigned, both as
President and as a member of SWANU. Gerson Hitjevi Veii
became Acting President (he was confirmed as SWANU
President in 1968) and the External Council was reorganised.[17]

SWAPO President Sam Nujoma had, in fact, pre-empted
Kozonguizi by returning to Namibia in March 1966. Nujoma
and Lucas Pohamba (then Assistant SWAPO Representative in
Zambia, now SWAPO Treasurer) decided to test claims by the

South African regime that Namibian nationalists abroad were in self-imposed exile and could return to the country. They also hoped to draw international attention to the situation in Namibia. They chartered a plane and flew to Windhoek on 20 March. The plane was detained, however, and they were immediately arrested. The following day they were escorted back on to the plane at gun-point and were deported to Zambia.

9 DEVELOPMENTS AT THE UNITED NATIONS & THE INTERNATIONAL COURT OF JUSTICE (1960s)

In the late 1950s and early 1960s there was intensive petitioning at the United Nations by and on behalf of Namibian nationalists, and a general belief that the best way to proceed towards Namibian independence was to place the country under UN trusteeship. Debates on Namibia at the UN were closely followed in the country. Apart from providing information to the world body, the contents of petitions were publicised at home and abroad and helped to win support for the cause of Namibian independence. The new international climate, with the progress of decolonisation and the entry of Third World nations into the UN, generated expectations that the UN could successfully establish its authority over Namibia. Some recalled that South African Prime Minister Verwoerd 'once said that the UN will not be allowed into Namibia'[1], but in May 1962 a special UN mission visited the country, fuelling expectations of change. In fact, many Namibians believed that 1963 would be the year of their freedom.

From 1958 to 1966, however, there was a general crisis of confidence in the UN, which led to the ending of South Africa's mandate over Namibia, and which was a factor in SWAPO's decision to launch an armed liberation struggle. This was mainly brought about by:

1 the failure of various UN committees on Namibia to deal effectively with the matter and, in particular, the outcome of the 1962 UN Mission to Namibia; and

2 the case brought against South Africa in the International Court of Justice by Liberia and Ethiopia and the Court's 1966 Judgement.

In 1958 the Good Offices Committee, under the Chairmanship of the former Governor of Ghana, Sir Charles Arden Clarke, suggested a plan to partition Namibia. The idea was essentially to split Namibia into a southern sector (including the fertile land, white settler farms and mineral resources) to be incorporated into South Africa, and a northern sector that South Africa would administer under a UN trusteeship agreement.

In 1960 the Committee on South West Africa tried to visit Namibia to investigate 'steps which would enable the indigenous inhabitants ... to achieve a wide measure of internal self-government designed to lead them to complete independence as soon as possible'.[2] South Africa refused the committee entry to Namibia and said that any attempt by the UN to cross into Namibia illegally would be regarded as an act of aggression. The committee therefore visited various African capitals and spoke to Namibian nationalists in exile. However, the British government refused visas for them to visit Botswana to talk to Namibian petitioners who had crossed the Kalahari specifically for that purpose.

In 1962 the Special Committee for South West Africa succeeded in visiting Namibia but was compromised by the joint statement it made with the South African regime. The purpose of the committee's visit was to bring about the withdrawal of South African military personnel, the repeal of racially discriminatory laws, release of political prisoners, and the holding of elections under UN supervision and control, for a legislative assembly. The mission was headed by Vittorio Carpio of the Philippines and Dr Martinez de Alva of Mexico. It met a wide cross-section of people, receiving written and oral testimony from Namibians in the country and statements from those abroad.

The South African regime insisted on a joint statement being made by the committee and themselves. Carpio fell suddenly and inexplicably ill while this was being prepared and the statement was released to the press without his approving it. It tried to gloss over the situation in Namibia and made no mention of South Africa's extension of the apartheid system to the country. Carpio later dissociated himself from the statement, but serious doubt was already cast on the ability of the UN to act decisively on Namibia when necessary.

THE 1960–6 ICJ NAMIBIA CASE

In 1959 African Foreign Ministers met in Monrovia, and one of the issues they discussed was Namibia. It was here that the suggestion was first made that the question of Namibia be referred to the International Court of Justice at The Hague, to settle finally the legal status of the country and South Africa's obligations to the UN and the people of Namibia. In December 1960 the UN General Assembly opened discussions on Namibia. The Liberian representative announced that the Liberian and Ethiopian governments had instituted proceedings against South Africa before the ICJ. These two countries were the prime movers as African members of the former League of Nations, under which the mandate over Namibia had been originally granted to South Africa.

The lawyer who acted on behalf of Liberia and Ethiopia was Ernest A Gross, former US Assistant Secretary of State (1947–9) and US delegate to the UN (1949–55), but he was soon criticised for failing to consult properly with his clients. He advised Ethiopia and Liberia that they should narrow their case down and base it 'on official documents, statutes and statements defining apartheid'[3] and then assume that the Court would follow the American legal principle which rejected any claim that people could be treated as 'separate but equal' as the proponents of apartheid claimed was the case. This approach failed to establish the reality of South African rule in Namibia and therefore failed to show that South Africa was violating the terms of the original mandate.

The case proceeded very slowly. From March to November 1965 the ICJ heard witnesses from South Africa but no Namibians were heard, not even the petitioners to the UN. Gross cross-examined the South Africans extensively – to the annoyance of some of the judges – but the court had no provisions to punish, and therefore prevent, false statements.

On 18 July 1966 the Court handed down a decision which refused to judge the substance of the case. The votes were equally divided, so it was by the President's casting vote that the court decided 'to reject the claims of the Empire of Ethiopia and the Republic of Liberia'.[4] The reason given for this was that Ethiopia and Liberia had 'no special right or interest' in bringing the case. They had, however, argued that they were acting on behalf of former members of the League of Nations.

This verdict came as a complete surprise to both sides in the case and to most observers: a ruling against South Africa had been expected. It also effectively contradicted all previous rulings by the ICJ on Namibia and implied that no individual state or states could raise the question of Namibia's status before the Court. The actual voting produced a stalemate, 7:7, so the Judge President, Sir Percy Spender of Australia (who had always taken a pro-South Africa line when he was Australian representative at the UN), voted twice to decide the issue.

The Liberian representative at the UN declared that the decision of the Court was 'the object of condemnation and a source of shock and disgust all over the entire world'.[5] Moreover, the credibility of the Court itself was brought into question:

> On 18 July 1966 the Court handed down what may prove to be its most controversial judgement ever, holding that it was unable to give a decision on the merits of the dispute because Ethiopia and Liberia had no legal right or interest in the subject matter of their complaints. By reaching this arid conclusion the Court signally failed to dispel widespread doubts about the relevance of its role in the settlement of critical international disputes; and at the same time it tragically deepened anxiety about the prospects of bringing this particular dispute to a just conclusion in the context of the international rule of law.[6]

Reactions by Namibian nationalists and the South African regime obviously differed widely. Both SWANU and SWAPO saw the decision as a miscarriage of justice, while the South African regime hailed it as a victory.

Only South Africa and the white settlers of South West Africa were jubilant: 'The bars in Windhoek stayed open all night', as one reporter wrote. Twenty years of efforts to change South Africa's attitude had gone by without results.[7]

At the UN, the General Assembly responded on 27 October 1966, in a move initiated by Ghana, and terminated the mandate. It declared that South Africa 'has no other right to administer the Territory and that henceforth South West Africa comes under the direct responsibility of the United Nations.'[8] It also established a UN body to administer the country until independence. This was the UN Council for South West Africa (now known as the UN Council for Namibia). It operates out of the UN headquarters in New York and now also has regional offices in Lusaka, Luanda and Gaborone, through which the UN channels material assistance to those Namibians residing in countries adjacent to Namibia.

10 THE LAUNCHING OF SWAPO'S ARMED STRUGGLE

By the mid- to late 1960s the method of armed struggle had been adopted by most nationalist movements in southern and Portuguese Africa. Angola led the way with a series of armed uprisings in 1961. This was followed by FRELIMO in Mozambique, which took up arms in 1964. After the 1965 Unilateral Declaration of Independence by the Smith regime in Rhodesia and Britain's failure to intervene decisively on behalf of the black population, ZANU took up arms in 1966. In 1967 the combined forces of the ANC of South Africa and ZAPU had their first military encounters with the Smith regime. For Namibians, however, the moment of truth came with the 1966 judgement, or non-judgement, of the ICJ. Any hopes or illusions about the will of the outside world to help them were dealt a heavy blow. Andimba Ja Toivo summed up Namibians' reactions as follows:

> The judgement of the World Court was a bitter disappointment to us. We felt betrayed and we believed that South Africa would never fulfil its trust. Some felt that we would secure our freedom only by fighting for it.[1]

SWAPO declared that

> The effect that it has on our people is that it relieves them once and for all from any illusions which they may have harboured about the United Nations as some kind of saviour in their plight . . . We have no alternative but to rise in arms and bring about our own liberation. The supreme test must be faced and we must at once begin to cross the many rivers of blood on our march towards freedom.[2]

In fact, SWAPO had been preparing itself for an armed struggle for some time, although it was hoped that a peaceful solution to Namibia's independence could still be found. In 1962 the first group of SWAPO members began military training. A number of them were then sent into Namibia in August 1965. They established a base at Omgulumbashe in Ovamboland, intending to train more people as fighters. The first group was of six men, under the leadership of John Otto

Nankuthu, but they were soon reinforced by other small units of fighters. The early strategy was summed up in the words of Tobias H Hainyeko, SWAPO's first military commander:

> Our guerrilla warfare will first start from the weak point – that is the countryside – where the development of means of transportation for the enemy is too weak to enable them to mobilise their forces. In these areas the enemy forces could face some logistical problems.[3]

The South Africans learnt of the presence of SWAPO fighters in the country and arrested some of them in Okavango in May 1966. They then planned a large-scale attack on the Omgulum-bashe base. Although the SWAPO fighters knew of the imminent attack, they decided to wait to meet the enemy. Thus it was that the first armed encounter between SWAPO and the South Africans took place at at Omgulumbashe on 26 August 1966. The South Africans claimed that they wiped out the camp, but Ja Toivo talks of two SWAPO men being killed, while the rest retreated or were captured.[4]

Almost two weeks after the battle of Omgulumbashe, on 6 September 1966, the South African Prime Minister Dr Verwoerd was assassinated. On 28 September the houses of two South African officials on the Namibia/Angola border were burned down by SWAPO fighters. In November and December, SWAPO raided the property of pro-South African chiefs in Ovamboland, taking arms and wounding their bodyguards.[5] Fears spread in Namibia among the whites that these events together meant a new onslaught on white supremacy.

In May 1967 the SWAPO military commander, Tobias Hainyeko, led a mission to investigate the situation in north-east Namibia (Caprivi). He wanted to improve communications between his operational headquarters in Tanzania and SWAPO's fighting units in Namibia. Hainyeko went to meet a colleague from Namibia at Sesheke, which straddles the Zambia/Namibia border. On his return, on 18 May 1967, he met his death in action against the South African forces patrolling the Zambezi river. SWAPO reported that he was betrayed to the South Africans by the local manager of the Caltex company that ran the barges from Katima Mulilo along the river.[6]

The news of Hainyeko's death reached SWAPO's Provisional Headquarters in Dar es Salaam two days later and caused considerable distress. As if in anticipation of what was to come, Hainyeko's last words when he left Dar es Salaam had been 'I will never surrender to an enemy. It is either him or me.'

Hainyeko's deputy, Leonard Phillemon, then became commander of SWAPO's fighters. Right from the start, however, there was a lot of uneasiness about Phillemon, especially amongst the younger fighters who questioned his activities in Namibia leading up to the battle of Omgulumbashe. A number of SWAPO fighters on different missions were captured by the South Africans as they entered Namibia, and this raised suspicions of there being a highly placed informer in SWAPO's military wing. Then in 1968 Phillemon was accused of working for the South African regime and was detained by SWAPO. Dimo Amambo took over as commander.[7]

THE 1967–8 TERRORISM TRIAL

Following the launching of the armed struggle, 37 SWAPO leaders and fighters were arrested, including Nathaniel Mahuilili (Acting President), John Ya Otto (Acting Secretary General), Andimba Ja Toivo (Regional Secretary for Ovamboland) and Jason Mutumbulua (Secretary for External Relations).[8] They were taken to Pretoria and detained there. At first they were held incommunicado under the Suppression of Communism Act, but the South African regime introduced new legislation in June 1967 – which has become known as the Terrorism Act – and made it retrospective to 1962 to cover SWAPO activities since that date.

The 37 Namibians were charged under this Act. They were severely tortured by the South African police while in detention. Ya Otto has described being given electric shocks even before the questioning began:

> When electricity tears through your body, you cannot think, let alone speak. I discovered that for the Special Branch this was the last stage of priming their detainees for co-operation – the last torture before sitting down to 'talk reason' . . . Each time it felt as if a bomb of a thousand sharp needles was exploding inside me, tearing my guts apart, pushing my eyes out from their sockets, bursting my skin open in a dozen places.[9]

Ja Toivo

> was blindfolded and handcuffed to a hot-water pipe; then wires were attached to various parts of his body and he was given electric shock. Threatening to crush his genitals while he was thus suspended, they mocked him and told

him, 'Here in Pretoria, we will make a new man of you. You will become young again' . . . 'Where is your United Nations now?' they jeered at him.[10]

The other detainees were also tortured. The defence attorney, Joel Carlson, took up the case of Gabriel Mbindi, a 68-year-old member who had worked at the Windhoek Post Office, and the South African regime unexpectedly settled the matter out of court. They paid Carlson's legal costs and £500 'extra' – an unstated admission of guilt – and released Mbindi.[11]

Eventually, the men were brought before the court in June 1967 and had their charges read out to them. Almost all were in a poor state of health. One of the men, Ephraim Kamati Kaporo, died in October 1967, during the trial. Several others had sustained serious injuries, either during detention or in the battle at Omgulumbashe.

The witnesses for South Africa were mainly policemen and members of the South African security forces responsible for monitoring SWAPO activities. There were also documents used to support the regime's case, some of which were stolen from the briefcase of SWAPO President Sam Nujoma while he was staying in London in 1966. The South Africans regarded Ja Toivo as an important leader and hoped to break him and turn him into a state witness. They also tried to turn Jason Mutumbulua. In both these attempts they failed, but they succeeded with the former SWAPO Vice-President, Louis Nelengani.

Nelengani had been suspended as Vice-President after being involved in a fight in December 1965 with Jacob Kuhangua, then SWAPO Secretary General. The two men fought physically and in the process Nelengani stabbed Kuhangua, who was paralysed from the waist down as a result of his injuries. A local court in Dar es Salaam found Nelengani not guilty of any charge because of provocation from Kuhangua. However, he soon returned to Namibia a disillusioned man. He was then badly tortured by the South Africans and forced to act as a state witness in the 1967 trial.

The defence case rested on the question of South Africa's jurisdiction over Namibia, and argued that the Terrorism Act could not be applied to Namibia, but the judge ruled that the court could not question the jurisdiction of the Act. At the end of the trial the defence team hoped that if the accused did not make any statements they might get lighter sentences. But they decided to make their views known on the trial and the whole question of South African rule in Namibia. Ja Toivo was elected to speak for the group. His speech had a great impact in many countries and has inspired Namibians to this day. Addressing the South African judge, he said:

> We are Namibians and not South Africans. We do not now, and will not in the future, recognise your right to govern us; to make laws for us in which we had no say; to treat our country as if it were your property and us as if you were our masters. We have always regarded South Africa as an intruder in our country . . .
> We claim independence for South West Africa. We do not expect that independence will end our troubles, but we do believe that our people are entitled – as are all peoples – to rule themselves . . . Even though I did not agree that people should go into the bush, I could not refuse to help them when I knew that they were hungry. I even passed on the request for dynamite . . . I was not, and I could not remain a spectator in the struggle of my people for their freedom.
> I am a loyal Namibian and I could not betray my people to their enemies. I admit that I decided to assist those who had taken up arms. I know that the struggle will be long and bitter. I also know that my people will wage that struggle, whatever the cost.[12]

Tuhadeleni Kahumba also spoke; he was one of the oldest defendants and an early volunteer for training at Omgulum-bashe:

> We find ourselves a conquered people, and the master does not discuss with the slave. And so we shall free ourselves and then discussion will again take place between equals.
> Our struggle against South Africa is an unequal one. I have seen the power of South Africa at Omgulumbashe. But David slew Goliath because he had right on his side, and we Namibians have faith that we, too, have right on our side.[13]

Twenty of the detainees, including Tuhadeleni, were sentenced to life imprisonment;[14] nine, including Ja Toivo, got twenty years;[15] Jonas Nashivela and Nathaniel Lot Homateni got five years. Ya Otto, Mutumbulua and Mahuilili were sentenced under the Suppression of Communism Act to five years, with four years and eleven months suspended. Matheus Joseph was discharged; Simeon Ipinge Iputa was acquitted. (Ephraim Kaporo died during the trial).

Eighty-one other SWAPO members had been named as co-conspirators in the Terrorism Trial. This included the SWAPO leadership abroad and some in Namibia, but in the end they were not brought to trial. A further indication of the South African regime's determination to repress nationalist activity in the wake of the launching of the armed struggle was the arrest in April 1967 of SWANU Acting President Hitjevi Veii. He was charged with sabotage for 'inciting, encouraging and instigating people to injure police informers, whites and members of the police force'. he had spoken at a meeting to resist the continuing forced removals of Namibians from Windhoek's Old Location to Katutura. Veii was tried in May 1967 and sentenced to five years on Robben Island.

11 1971–2: A TURNING POINT

In 1970, fearing that the authority of the UN was being undermined, the Security Council set up an Ad Hoc Sub-Committee to explore ways of implementing UN rulings on Namibia. This committee decided to take the Namibia case back to the ICJ and ask the Court what the legal consequences were for UN member states of the continued presence of South Africa in Namibia. There was considerable opposition to this idea at first from the Africa group at the UN and from SWAPO – they feared another unsatisfactory ruling, like that of 1966, which could only strengthen the hand of South Africa. Informal behind-the-scenes consultations had, however, revealed that, partly because the composition of the judges had changed since 1966, a ruling in favour of the Namibian people was likely.[1]

When the ICJ took up the case, South Africa attempted to delay the proceedings by offering to supply information to the Court, It also asked to be allowed to hold a plebiscite in Namibia to determine the wishes of the people. The Court would not entertain this, however. SWAPO lobbied informally at the Court and was allowed an observer delegation in the courtroom. No member state spoke up for South Africa – a symptom of that country's increasing international isolation, Then in June 1971 the Court concluded its hearing and the judges gave the following verdict:

> The Court is of opinion . . .
> 1 that, the continued presence of South Africa in Namibia being illegal, South Africa is under obligation to withdraw its administration from Namibia immediately and thus put an end to its occupation of the Territory . . .
> 2 that member states of the United Nations are under obligation to recognize the illegality of South Africa's presence in Namibia and the invalidity of its acts on behalf of or concerning Namibia, and to refrain from any acts and in particular any dealings with the Government of South Africa implying recognition of the legality of, or

lending support or assistance to, such presence and administration.[2]

Finally, the weight of international legal opinion had come down in favour of the nationalist cause of the Namibian people.

The UN Security Council met in September-October 1971 to discuss the ICJ Opinion. Both South Africa and SWAPO addressed the meeting, with SWAPO President Sam Nujoma becoming the first leader of an African nationalist movement, still campaigning for independence, to do so. Nujoma called upon the Security Council to live up to its responsibility over Namibia. But South Africa rejected the Opinion and the South African Administrator in Namibia, Mr Van Der Watt, said simply 'We will continue to govern South West Africa as in the past.'[3]

Other Namibian groups, such as SWANU and the Herero Chief's Council, expressed satisfaction at the finding of the Court. Jariretundu Kozonguizi stated that the Opinion provided 'the necessary, but at no time in doubt, legal basis for the just struggle of the people of Namibia'.[4] Of particular significance is the endorsement and the welcome given by the churches to the ICJ Opinion. Bishop Colin Winter, head of the Anglican church in the country, described the way people in Windhoek reacted to the news: 'The decision at The Hague caused a sensation in Namibia. There was dancing in the African location.'[5]

South Africa was determined to pursue its idea of some form of a plebiscite to gauge the opinions of Namibians. To do this, they went to the biggest church in the country – the Evangelical Lutheran Ovambo-Kavango church (ELOK) – and its Bishop, Leonard Auala, distributed a questionnaire throughout congregations in Ovamboland asking people their views on the ICJ Opinion. The result shattered South Africa's illusions about popular support for its policies:

> South Africa has never since offered a plebiscite to decide on the continuance of South African rule. When asked, in their own language, by people they trusted, for their opinion on the world ruling, the people of Ovamboland returned an overwhelming vote: they totally rejected the continuance of white rule from South Africa.[6]

This was followed by an Open Letter to the South African Prime Minister Vorster from Bishop Auala and Moderator Pastor Gowaseb, head of the Evangelical Lutheran church

(ELK). It conveyed Bishop Auala's findings and condemned South African rule:

> Our people are not free and by the way they are treated, they do not feel safe . . . The Church Boards' urgent wish is that in terms of the declaration of the World Court and in co-operation with the UNO . . . your government will seek a peaceful solution to the problems of our land and will see to it that human rights be put into operation and that South West Africa may become a self-sufficient and independent state.[7]

This was the first time the black leaders of the churches in Namibia had taken a public stand of this sort in support of the demand for freedom. It was to be the first of many such stands and it led to closer relations between the churches and increasing co-ordination of their work.

THE 1971–2 STRIKE

The effect of the ICJ Opinion within Namibia was very clear. Here was the international support that Namibians had wanted so long – a clear statement that South Africa's continued presence in the country was illegal. This was a fertile climate for political activists and a renewed nationalist campaign would not have been much of a surprise at that time. The major strike that swept through the country from December 1971 was, however, a new element in Namibian opposition to South African rule.

The strike began amongst contract workers – the most exploited group of Namibian workers. The spark that started it off was lit by a comment by the South African Commissioner for Indigenous People in Namibia, Jannie de Wet. In response to growing public criticism of the harsh and binding nature of the contract labour system, de Wet stated that it was not a form of slavery because the workers signed their contracts 'voluntarily'.[8] In so doing, he touched the nerve of people already full of anger at the way their lives were brutalised by this system. The response was, therefore, immediate.

Letters were exchanged at the beginning of December between contract workers in Windhoek, Walvis Bay and Tsumeb, sharing ideas on how to organise a strike. One of these read as follows:

67

We have decided to break the contract. On Monday we must not go to work or eat in the [communal] kichen. Those who disagree with this must leave or they will be hurt. Those who work at night must not return to the compound.[9]

A strike diary kept by Leonard Nghipandulua, one of the strike leaders, shows how the plans developed. Monday 13 December was determined in advance as the day the strike was to start. When that day came, 6,000 men in the contract workers' compound in Katutura went on strike. The compound was surrounded by the police and the gates were sealed with the workers inside. By the end of that week, the strike had spread to Walvis Bay and to the Tsumeb, Klein Aub and Oamites copper mines. The Berg Aukas lead and vanadium mine and Uis tin mine were also affected. Later in the month, workers at the Consolidated Diamond Mines in Oranjemund joined the strike. Many workers in commercial and industrial concerns and on some farms also left their work:

> According to the South African government, the strike at its peak involved 13,000 workers. Unofficial estimates, however, put the number at over 20,000 – close to half the Ovambo contract labour force.[10]

The South African regime immediately arrested those whom they regarded as the strike ring-leaders. Then they sent all strikers back to the reserves, in this case mostly to northern Namibia. In fact, relying on the subsistence agricultural production of their families in the reserves was the only way the strikers could hope to survive the strike physically and economically. An ad hoc strike committee led by Johannes Nangutuuala was then set up. A mass meeting of 3,500 workers held at Oluno, near Ondangua, on 10 January 1972 drew up a long list of demands, which included an end to the whole contract labour system; freedom to choose jobs according to skill and interest and to leave a job if so desired; freedom for a worker to have his family with him or visit his family; salaries to be set in accordance with skill and irrespective of colour.[11]

The South African regime reacted by sending armed police into Ovamboland. Police intimidation, arrests and even killings were reported. Within the industrial centres there was an attempt to get other Namibian workers to take the places of the strikers, but largely without success:

> Panic spread through the white community as not only mines and businesses were being threatened. Goods were

piling up in the railways, litter and garbage went uncoll-
ected, there were no deliveries of milk, and other essential
services were threatened. White schoolboys, largely teen-
agers, were hired to haul garbage at wages of over R100
(US$140) a month – ten times what black adult workers
received for the same work. The whites saw nothing
incongruous in this.[12]

Discussions were held between the South African regime, the
recruiting agency, South West Africa Native Labour Association (SWANLA), and major employers, and a new scheme for
the recruitment of workers was agreed upon. In practice,
however, it was simply a change of terminology – the rigid
reality of the contract remained intact. SWANLA was replaced
by labour bureaux run by the tribal authorities set up by South
Africa; the words 'master' and 'servant' were replaced by
'employer' and 'employee'; working hours were to be stip-
ulated; it would be easier to change jobs; and there was a
promise that workers would be able to maintain contact with
their families.

The national press and radio were used by the South African
regime to claim that the strikers had, in fact, won major
concessions and that Nangutuuala had personally agreed to the
new deal, although it has never been clear whether he
voluntarily did so. Then a news black-out was imposed on
northern Namibia. Strikers began to register under the 'new'
contract, but found it hardly any different from the old, and the
unrest began to increase. White women and children in the
northern regions were evacuated to the south of the country.
South African troops were sent in for the first time and
Portuguese troops moved south across the border with Angola
to assist them. Strike meetings were broken up and fired on,
and people rounded up en masse. On 4 February a state of
emergency was declared in Ovamboland under Proclamation
R17: meetings were banned; no 'unauthorised' person was
allowed to visit the area; political organisation, boycotts,
'subversive' statements, etc. became imprisonable offences;
and the police were empowered to detain indefinitely without
charge anyone suspected of an offence. R17 remained in force
until 1977 when other security legislation affecting the whole
country replaced it.

The twelve contract workers and one student who had been
arrested at the beginning of the strike were brought to trial in
January 1971. They were charged with intimidating and
inciting others to strike and breaking their own contracts by

striking. Many international observers attended the trial and, in the end, eight strikers were fined and the others acquitted. The magistrate was obliged to acknowledge the appalling pay and conditions revealed by the trial.

Bishop Winter and his family had openly sided with the strikers and those on trial, and they were deported from Namibia in March 1972. By the end of March most strikers had gone back to work. The open brutality of the South African regime and the way they undermined and compromised the leader of the strike committee, Nangutuuala, helped to break the strike. The thousands of extra people in the north also overstretched the meagre resources of most families and sheer poverty helped to force the men back to work.

The strike itself was organised by ordinary workers, most of whom had litle formal education. OPO, and then SWAPO, had, however, been organising amongst the contract workers for over a decade. Many of the strikers were SWAPO members or supporters, and SWAPO was clearly involved in the strike. Nevertheless, SWAPO Acting President Nathaniel Mahuilili has said:

> The Ovambos know of the World Court decision on South West Africa, they know the feelings in the United Nations.They realise that the eyes of the world are on South West Africa. Not only SWAPO, many other organisations and individuals regarded the contract labour system as a form of slave labour.[13]

This was the first time that workers in Namibia had laid down their tools not only in demand of better pay or conditions, but to demand that the contract labour system itself be abolished. The mere fact that the strike got off the ground was an organisational achievement within the context of South African rule in Namibia. Important too was the involvement of many Namibian workers who were not contract workers, and the participation of the families of strikers – mostly subsistence agriculturalists – who were politicised by the strike.

Many of the workers who had been involved in the strike then turned to wider political activity and some went on to play an important role in the political mobilisation campaign conducted by the SWAPO Youth League in 1973–5. This clearly shows the politicising effect of the strike. People initially acted in response to their immediate experience, e.g. the contract labour system which dominated their lives. In the course of the strike, however, and perhaps partly because they did not achieve their objectives, they gained wider perspectives, realising that, in order to bring about the changes they desired, they had to strive for much wider political change.

12 SOUTH AFRICA'S BANTUSTAN POLICIES & NATIONALIST RESPONSES

In 1962 the Odendaal Commission of Inquiry, so named after its chairman, was established by South Africa to recommend a plan for the development of Namibia 'and more particularly its non-white inhabitants', within the context of 'what has already been planned and put into practice'.[1] Its report came out in 1963,[2] arguing strongly for the 'separate development' of black and white in Namibia, that is, a 'further extension of the system of apartheid throughout the Territory; and to make it the basic principle of political, economic and social organisation, as in South Africa'.[3]

Eleven black authorities were proposed, through which Namibians would be separated along ethnic lines from each other and from the whites. The Coloureds, all urban dwellers, were to have a Council; the Rehobothers would retain their traditional area and Council (Raad). For the other black groups there would be homelands, conceived as separate 'states' with their own legislative councils. They were to be given extra land but essentially they covered the same areas as the existing African reserves, much of them dry and barren (see Map 8). The consolidation of the various black communities into these homelands would be achieved by the removal of thousands of Namibians from their existing homes. The remaining 'white area' would comprise the good farming land, the mines and diamond areas, towns and economic infrastructure.

The 'white area' would be administered by a white legislative assembly which would have powers over white education and health services, roads, local authorities and townships, public works, personal tax and income tax. All black health and educational services, transport, taxation, etc. were to fall directly under South African ministries. In effect, though, the health and educational facilities proposed for blacks were pitiful; there were to be no pension schemes for blacks and the old and destitute were simply sent to the homelands. The affairs of blacks living in the urban areas were to be regulated by delegates from the homeland to which they were allocated.[4]

This was to be an even closer integration of Namibia into South Africa, a dismembering of the country totally at odds with South Africa's mandate to administer the territory. Indeed

Table 2 *Bantustan Structures up to 1977*

Whites	Exclusively white Legislative Assembly
Ovambo	Legisative Assembly 1968, Self-Governing Territory 1973
Kavango	Legislative Assembly 1970, Self-Governing Territory 1973
Damara	Damara Advisory Council 1971, expanded powers 1977
Caprivi	Legislative Assembly 1972
Rehobothers	Self-Governing Territory 1976, elected 'Kaptein' 1977
Coloured	Partially elected Coloured Council 1961
Nama	Nama Council 1976
Tswana	No legislative or advisory bodies
Ovakuruvehi (Bushmen)	No legislative or advisory bodies
Herero	No legislative assembly

the Odendaal Report explicitly stated that 'the Government of South Africa no longer regards the original mandate as still existing as such.'[5]

There was widespread opposition within Namibia to these proposals, but South Africa went ahead with legislation that would allow them to be implemented, passing the Development of Self-Government for Native Nations in South West Africa Act in 1968 and the South West Africa Affairs Act in 1969. The Odendaal Plan has formed the basis of South Africa's policy towards Namibia ever since then. Table 2 shows the evolution of these Bantustan structures in Namibia up to 1977.

THE 1972 UN MISSION TO NAMIBIA

At the height of the 1971–2 strike the UN Security Council held a special session in Addis Ababa and passed a resolution calling on the Secretary General to establish negotiations that would lead to self-determination for the people of Namibia. This led to a visit to Namibia by Dr Kurt Waldheim in March 1972. Nothing was immediately achieved by the visit, however, and Waldheim appointed a representative, Dr A Escher, to continue negotiations on his behalf. In October 1972 Escher led another mission to Namibia and accepted South African proposals for an Advisory Council to be set up, with representatives drawn from the various regions. However, he failed to commit South Africa to clarifying its own interpretation of self-determination for Namibia and did not challenge Vorster's claim that this could only be done once Namibians had more experience in 'self-government'. The South Africans exploited similarities in terminology to cover their very different political approach. South Africa was committed to 'self-determination for the peoples' of Namibia, and the UN to 'self-determination of the people'.[6]

The Advisory Council was set up in March 1973. South African Prime Minister Vorster appointed a Special Representative, Billy Marais, to run it, but it was clearly envisaged as fitting into existing Bantustan structures and the 'regional' representatives were chosen on an ethnic basis. Two people were nominated by the all-white legislative assembly; and two Tswana, two Ovakuruvehi (Bushmen) representatives and two representatives from each of the Ovambo, Kavango and East Caprivian Bantustan governments or councils were appointed by the South African regime. SWAPO, SWANU and Herero Chief Clemens Kapuuo rejected the council. Chief Munjuku Nguvauva of the Mbanderu group of the Hereros, and representatives of the Rehoboth, Nama and Damara communities attended as observers, although Chief Munjuku soon walked out, saying that he wanted independence for the country as a whole. South Africa stated that the council was still in a 'formative stage'[7] and continued with its Bantustan programme and Bantustan elections in Ovamboland later in 1973.

THE 1973 OVAMBOLAND ELECTION BOYCOTT

In 1973 the South African regime introduced the Self-Government for Native Nations in South West Africa Amendment Act. This provided the basis for elections to be held in the Bantustans, leading to their attainment of so-called self-governing status. Through such moves South Africa hoped to deflect nationalist and international pressure on it to withdraw from Namibia.

In 1973 elections were held for legislative assemblies in Ovamboland and Okavango. They were immediately opposed by the Namibian people, however. Especially active were the SWAPO Youth League (SYL) and the newly formed Democratic Co-operative Party (DEMKOP), led by Johannes Nangutuuala who had earlier headed the ad hoc contract workers' committee. DEMKOP had some following in Ovamboland and amongst contract workers, but it has since become defunct.

74

A campaign to boycott the elections was launched, in the form of meetings and rallies, although these were expressly forbidden under the terms of Proclamation R17 (the exceptions being church services and meetings called by South African or Bantustan officials). Those leading the boycott pointed out that the very existence of such regulations made it impossible for the elections to be free. However, their central argument was to oppose South Africa's overall Bantustan policy and demand independence for a unitary Namibian state. The motto 'One Namibia, One Nation' was widely adopted. On 30 April 1973 John Ya Otto, SWAPO's Acting Secretary General, and Johannes Nangutuuala and Andreas Nuukwawo of DEMKOP addressed one such rally in Ovamboland. A few days later they were arrested. Then followed a spate of arrests of DEMKOP and SWAPO Youth League members by the South African authorities.

There was also increased conflict between the South African regime and the churches. Bishop Auala of ELOK and the leaders of the Anglican and Catholic churches opposed the Ovamboland election. The only church leader to support the elections was Revd P. Kalangula of the Ovambo Independent Church – a group that had broken away from the Anglican church in opposition to Bishop Winter's radical leadership.[8] ELOK put out a news-letter called *Omukuetu* (Friend) which voiced the churches' rejection of these elections. In May 1973 a bomb destroyed the ELOK printing press at Oniipa where *Omukuetu* was produced, and Bishop Auala held the South Africans responsible for this.[9]

When the elections took place on 1st and 2nd August the result was a victory for the nationalist cause. Only 2.5% of those elgible to vote (1,300 out of 50,000) did so, and many of these were the Bantustan policemen and officials.[10] In Okavango, where the boycott campaign never really took off, the percentage poll in the September 1973 elections was 66.2%.[11] The South African regime tried to make their own propaganda out of the results, and the Commissioner General Jannie de Wet claimed that this proved that 'a modern election was completely foreign to the Ovambos.'[12]

THE 1975 OVAMBOLAND ELECTIONS

A second set of elections took place in Ovamboland in January 1975 to increase the number of elected members of the legislative assembly from 21 to 42. The South Africans' decision to hold these elections has been explained as an attempt by de Wet to erase the successful boycott of 1973.[13] This time the turn-out was 55%. Of those eligible to vote within Ovamboland, 70% did so. But only 4.2% of those eligible Ovambos living and working elsewhere in the country voted.

These results were hailed by South Africa as a major victory over SWAPO. Chief Elifas, Chief Minister of Ovamboland, 'accepted the result ... as a vote of confidence in himself and his government, and as a mandate for action against certain individuals, including churchmen, on grounds of incitement.'[14] Elifas was, however, hated by many Namibians. Only seven months after the elections, on 16 August 1975, he was assassinated by a gunshot when leaving a bar.

SWAPO and DEMKOP had called for a boycott of the 1975 elections as well, but the determination of the South African regime not to repeat the experience of 1973 led to widespread intimidation of people in Ovamboland:

> Many armoured vehicles and infantry reinforcements made their appearance in Ovamboland ... The labour recruitment at Oluno was approached and approximately 2,000–3,000 men who sought recruitment for work in the South were told that they would never be recruited unless they voted ... Clerks were of course under obligation to vote ... Chief Josia Taapopi of Uukwaludhi ... said that nobody would be allowed to cultivate any maize or grains without crossing the ballot paper ... the tribal police, armed with .303 guns, rubber batons and tribal swords, forced people from their homes and escorted them to the polls ... The old, blind and disabled, as well as mentally retarded people, who receive pensions from the government, were told they would lose their pensions.[15]

Moreover, there had been a vicious campaign by the South African regime since 1973 to break Namibian resistance to their policies. SWAPO and DEMKOP had been greatly weakened by a campaign of floggings, trials and victimisation of their members. Partly as a result of this repression, there had been an exodus of thousands of SWAPO members and activists who left Namibia in 1974. Had it not been for these factors, 'the Ovambo result could not have been attained.'[16]

13 POLITICAL TRIALS

After the 1973 Ovamboland election, teachers, students and nurses continued to protest against the newly reconstituted Bantustan authorities. Meetings were held all over Namibia, with the SWAPO Youth League playing a leading role. The Ovamboland Bantustan authorities responded by trying to repress this opposition. Hundreds of men and women, of all ages, were rounded up. They were accused of being members of SWAPO, using the name 'Namibia', singing SWAPO songs, attending SWAPO meetings, wearing SWAPO colours (red, green and blue), and thereby undermining the Ovamboland Bantustan government, even though SWAPO was at no time declared illegal or banned. The sentences imposed included fines, loss of the right to trade or seek work outside Ovamboland, and public floggings.[1]

The flogging was done using a branch of the Malakani palm: twenty to thirty strokes were administered to the naked buttocks or back. The South African regime claimed that this was a traditional form of punishment, so they could not intervene. This has, however, been vigorously denied by Namibians and by anthropologists. One woman described the flogging thus:

> I was asked why I had joined SWAPO, to which I replied that I had joined because it struggled for our betterment . . . Rachel was the first to be flogged. She was compelled to lie over a chair in the 'hall', in full view of all the members gathering, of men, women and children. 4 Policemen each held her by a limb, and she was flogged by a tribal Policeman . . . I was flogged in the same way. After my flogging, I . . . walked as if I was crippled, and I state that I have never endured such extreme pain in all my life . . . At no stage was a charge put to me, and to this day I have no understanding of my alleged offence.[2]

Bishop Richard Wood (who led the Anglican church in Namibia after Bishop Winter was deported), Bishop Auala of ELOK and Thomas Kamati (a student and SWAPO member) initiated a series of actions in the Supreme Court in Namibia to try to bring a halt to the floggings. Their evidence was based on a number of sworn affidavits by people who had been flogged, and other relevant persons, such as doctors, church leaders, etc. They won a temporary interdict prohibiting the floggings from November 1973 to March 1974. But their application was then dismissed. In February 1975, however, the South African Supreme Court in Bloemfontein upheld an appeal against this and ordered the Ovamboland authorities to stop arresting, detaining or inflicting punishment on anyone just because he/she was suspected of being a member of DEMKOP or SWAPO.[3] The floggings also aroused widespread international condemnation and focused international attention once more on Namibia.

THE SWAPO YOUTH LEAGUE TRIALS

From 1973–5 there was a series of trials of SWAPO Youth League (SYL) members and leaders. The defendants used the courtroom, however, as a platform for fervent political speeches and succeeded in mobilising more support for SWAPO and the nationalist cause within Namibia and internationally.

John Ya Otto, Johannes Nangutuuala and Andreas Nuuk-wawo, who had been arrested at the end of April 1973, were charged with addressing an illegal meeting. On Sunday 12 August a crowd of 3,000 people marched on the magistrate's court at Ondangua where the three were to be tried. A riot broke out, with many people getting hurt and/or being arrested. Ya Otto was sentenced to six months' imprisonment but he appealed. While this was being considered he was rearrested on similar charges and had to report every day to the police.

That same Sunday a peaceful rally, with speeches, songs and prayers, was held in Katutura by the SYL. The SWAPO flag was hoisted and a squad of over twenty youths was introduced to the meeting as Namibian 'policemen' appointed to keep order. The rally has been described as the highest point of the SYL's political campaign: the audience 'of more than two thousand five hundred spectators' was the greatest known in Namibian history.[4] One of the speakers told the crowd:

> For those of you who say the United Nations will bring freedom I just want to say that no day will dawn when the United Nations will bring them freedom. Namibians, till when will you carry on looking at how the Boers shed the blood of your brothers? Every Namibian must join in the struggle for freedom. We must not be frightened by this

blood which is being spilt. You must know that this freedom for Namibians will come through our own strength . . . All Namibians must stand up like one man so that the Boer Government be broken here in Namibia . . . and the last thing is, young people of Namibia, we must get into politics.[5]

As some people returned from the meeting to the contract workers' compound in Katutura, they found that they were locked out. They broke down the compound gates, the police arrived, and many people were arrested. In the following few weeks SYL leaders were arrested, public meetings banned and the police embarked on a house-to-house search of Windhoek for SYL activists. One young SWAPO supporter, Benjamin Phineas, was killed by the police. The SYL attempted to organise a strike but those who stayed at home were intimidated into going back to work. Protests spread beyond Katutura, however, with meetings being held in Walvis Bay and other centres. Schools were restive and students walked out of the Augustineum (the biggest state-run secondary school, then based in Okahandja).

By the end of August 1973 SYL leaders Jerry Ekandjo (Chairman), Jacob Ngidinua (Vice-Chairman), David Shikomba and Martin Kapewasha were in detention charged under the Sabotage Act, which 'has taken the precaution of equating utterances with acts of sabotage'.[6] When they came to trial in Swakopmund, SWAPO supporters filled the courtroom. Ngidinua summed up the defendants' attitude to their trial:

We have sabotaged nothing. We are oppressed. The people in Namibia who do sabotage are the Whites of South Africa. The court is here illegally and terrorises us in our own land. Only the United Nations may hear us. We do not recognise this court and we will be back.[7]

They were each sentenced to eight years' imprisonment and sent to Robben Island.

In January 1974, Eliakim Andreas was charged and sentenced to two years' imprisonment for inciting racial hostility at the meeting on the 12 August 1973. Eshriel Taapopi, who had taken over as SYL Chairman when Ekandjo was arrested, Joseph Kashea (SYL Acting Secretary), and Shihepo Iimbili (Treasurer), were arrested and charged with incitement to murder, public violence and arson. They had written a letter to SWAPO President Sam Nujoma calling for SWAPO's military wing to liberate Namibia. In March 1974, David

Shikomba, also charged with sabotage, was tried, sentenced to six years' imprisonment and sent to Robben Island.

SWAPO Chairman, David Meroro, and over 100 SWAPO members and supporters were arrested on their way to a meeting in January 1974. They were released after paying fines but Meroro was redetained in February along with SWAPO's Organising Secretary, Axel Johannes, and SYL official Thomas Kamati. The three were held under Section 6 of the Terrorism Act.

Meroro was physically and psychologically tortured. He was kept in solitary confinement for five months and suffered terrifying hallucinations. When finally brought to trial, the charges rested on his possession of banned literature, and he was sentenced to two months' imprisonment, conditionally suspended. Afraid that he would be arrested again, he left the country in 1975 to join SWAPO's work abroad. John Ya Otto, tipped off that the security police were looking for him yet again, left Namibia in June 1974.

Taapopi and Kashea were tried in June 1974. The state's evidence centred on their letter to Nujoma, which ran as follows:

> 1974 must be a year of sacrifice for Freedom and a year of the Realisation of the Power of SWAPO, not only abroad, but also inside Namibia. We must not wait on the UNO to bring us Freedom on a plate. We must rely on the Power we wield in Solidarity with our Brothers of Independent African states ... June, this year must be the month of Namibia's freedom. Until when are you waiting for somebody to free us? SWAPO's liberation Army must now fight the Boers and free Namibia before June. We promised the people that Namibia is to be free this year and now they are waiting for this freedom to come. Don't make us liars all in any possible way.[8]

Iimbili was called as the state's witness but once in the court he explained that the letter had been to persuade Nujoma to get the UN to act, saying 'the style which SWAPO had taught us is to fight with our mouths not with sticks or anything like that.'[9] But only that part of Iimbili's evidence that implicated the defendants was accepted by the court and Kashea and Taapopi were sentenced to five years' imprisonment, three of which were unconditionally suspended. They spent two years on Robben Island. As they left the court, Taapopi exclaimed 'I am off to college. There I will meet our head boy Ja Toivo.'[10]

Thomas Kamati, who had been flogged in Ovamboland in 1973 and was one of those who applied through the courts for the floggings to stop, spent several months in solitary confinement. He was eventually tried for scratching 'One Namibia, One Nation' on his cell wall. He suffered more in solitary confinement from 'seemingly endless misery and despair' than he had from the pain of the floggings.[11]

Axel Johannes was also held in solitary confinement, for the first six months of 1974, and then charged with assisting someone to leave the country. The case was eventually dropped but Johannes was physically assaulted by the security police and, at one time, attempted suicide while in detention, such was his 'anguish'.[12]

THE SWAKOPMUND TRIAL

Immediately following the assassination of Chief Elifas in August 1975 over 200 men and women, most of them SWAPO members, were detained by the South African regime, which held SWAPO responsible for the killing. These included Aaron Muchimba (SWAPO's Organising Secretary), Sam Shivute (SWAPO's Secretary in the north), Reuben Hauwanga, arrested three days before he was due to leave for the USA to study medicine, and Hendrik Shikongo, a SWAPO member who had left the bar minutes before Elifas was killed. Other SWAPO executive committee members who were detained were Skinny Hilundwa, Victor Nkandi, Otniel Kaakunga, Pejavi Elifas Muniaro, Johannes Nakawa and Alpheus Naruseb. Several churchmen, including Pastor Zephania Kameeta, then Principal of the Lutheran Theological College at Otjimbingwe and leading exponent of black liberation theology in Namibia, and Pastors Titus Ngula and Josefat Shangala were also arrested.

It has never been proven who killed Elifas, although after a long trial Muchimba and Shikongo were sentenced to death for being connected with the plot. Two nurses – Rauna Nambinga and Anna Nghihondjua – were also sentenced to five years' imprisonment for being accomplices. Moreover, at the time there were suggestions in Namibia that the South Africans might have been responsible:

> Two reasons were being advanced as to why his [Elifas's] death could have been engineered by the South Africans themselves. One was because it enabled them to detain people in connection with enquiries into his death. The other was . . . that in normal circumstances if a person is

81

killed while outside another man's house the first person you question is the owner of that house. This was apparently not done in this case.[13]

South Africa did, indeed, use Elifas's death and what became known as the Swakopmund trial to intimidate and frighten Namibian nationalists. Victor Nkandi was brought to the court to appear as a state witness. But when he appeared he testified that he had been tortured and refused to implicate his colleagues. Nkandi underwent what was essentially a trial within a trial. He and Axel Johannes, who the South Africans also tried to turn into a state witness (without success), were repeatedly detained and tortured and not finally released until 1978.[14]

In the trial itself

a considerable part of the judgement was devoted to an analysis of the evidence on SWAPO, its history, documents, songs and weapons. The court remarked that the 1966 draft Constitution of the organisation contained no references or profession that God through his omnipotence guides and controls the destiny of man.[15]

The defence team felt that from the start their every move was known to the prosecution. Suspecting a leak, one of the team of instructing lawyers, Colin du Preez, challenged other employees at the Lorentz and Bone law firm. He found that the switchboard and telex operator, Mrs Ellis, had passed defence documents on to the security police. This infiltration 'struck at the root of legal privilege: beyond justice, justice needed to be seen to be done'.[16] An appeal was successfully launched on this basis and, in an unprecedented ruling in South Africa's Supreme Court in Bloemfontein in February 1977, the convictions and death sentences were set aside. The Supreme Court judge, Chief Justice Rumpff (who had sent Ja Toivo and others to Robben Island a decade earlier) found that the grossness of the 'irregularity' could 'scarcely be surpassed'.[17]

What was intended to strike a blow at the heart of Namibian nationalism ultimately strengthened it. The release of Muchimba, Shikongo and the two nurses was greeted by jubilant crowds in Windhoek. It was seen as a victory for SWAPO and the Namibian nationalist cause.

EXODUS OF SWAPO MEMBERS

The Portuguese revolution by the Armed Forces Movement (AFM) of 25 April 1974 had far-reaching consequences for

Southern Africa, including Namibia. Although the situation in Angola was not transformed overnight, here was a neighbouring country which was no longer hostile to the nationalist aspirations of the Namibian people. The strict border control previously enforced by both Portuguese and South African authorities was relaxed, at least on the Angolan side. South African troops continued to patrol the Namibia/Angola border, but they could by no means seal it entirely.

The opportunity this provided for Namibians to flee the repression of the South African regime was not lost. There was an immediate exodus of Namibians from June 1974 onwards. Most of those leaving were from Ovamboland, where the repression was most widespread, and the region lost many of its skilled people – teachers, nurses, clerks and students. About 2,500 left in five months; most of them were young and 20% were women.[18]

The exodus caused a crisis for the South African regime as it badly affected the running of the Ovamboland Bantustan and disrupted essential services in the area, such as the church-run schools and hospitals. But SWAPO was also affected by the loss of so many leading members and activists.

Most of those who left went through Angola to Zambia, where SWAPO's provisional headquarters were. Once in exile they came under SWAPO's care. This had a significant effect on SWAPO's external organisation, as well as on the armed struggle.

In the early years of the armed struggle, it was through the Caprivi Strip that SWAPO fighters gained access to Namibia from training and rear bases in East Africa. SWAPO forces in the 1960s were relatively small in number and their activities were confined to small-scale encounters with the South African armed forces. They operated in small groups and were armed with light weapons. The most common operational tactics were to ambush South African forces and patrols and attack installations such as telephone lines and police stations.

Before they launched any operations in a particular area, the SWAPO fighters would campaign politically in that area. There was already a favourable political climate of support in Eastern Caprivi since the Caprivi African National Union (CANU) had joined SWAPO in 1964 and a number of young local SWAPO members left the country to undergo military training. Local assistance included information about movements of South African forces, and some provision of food and shelter. This close interaction between SWAPO fighters and the local people meant that the fighters would know the layout of the area before they undertook any military action. They were also immensely assisted by their knowledge of local languages.

Like the FLN in Algeria and other nationalist organisations in Southern Africa, SWAPO's armed struggle was based on classic guerrilla tactics. The close connections between political and military strategy, the emphasis on 'irregular' warfare, preserving one's own forces from direct encounters with the enemy, to deploy them in surprise attacks that had a good chance of success, were all features of SWAPO's armed struggle, as they were elsewhere in Africa. Mao Tse Tung has described such tactics as follows:

Disperse the forces among the masses to arouse them, and concentrate the forces to deal with the enemy.

The enemy advances, we retreat; the enemy halts, we harass; the enemy tires, we attack; the enemy retreats, we pursue.[1]

SWAPO fighters were initially trained within Africa (Egypt, Ghana, Algeria and Tanzania) and the Soviet Union. From 1965 onwards some fighters also went to China and North Korea. Then the fighters were brought together in Tanzania for orientation to harmonise and agree upon final operational procedures that were appropriate for Namibia. When they were sent to the front they went in small units. But there were enormous problems to be overcome in the late 1960s, just to get to the front in Namibia:

> We had to walk a long distance from Zambia through Angola. Some of our people also died in Angola and some missions could not reach Namibia, because they had to fight through Angola . . . The battles we were involved in, most of them were in Angola with the Portuguese . . . but even the South African soldiers were also involved in Angola and really we worked hard because by then we had to train the new recruits and we also had to fight to get food as we had to walk long distances and then we had to try and get transport, also after a battle then you must have more ammunition . . . I could say by the time we crossed into Namibia we were a bit tired but a bit more experienced.[2]

In October 1968 the South African Deputy Minister of Police acknowledged the growing 'threat' from SWAPO fighters on Namibia's northern borders, where 'literally hundreds' of trained men were waiting to enter the country:

> They were using new tactics. In the past, men had crossed the border heavily armed, using their weapons to terrorise the local inhabitants. Now they were coming unarmed, avoiding clashes with the police, and attempting to influence chiefs and others to co-operate with them.[3]

By 1969 SWAPO was operating in four regions – Ovamboland and Okavango, Kaokoveld, the Caprivi Strip, and Grootfontein in the central part of Namibia. By 1971 the Caprivi Strip was 'intensely patrolled by [South African] policemen and troops doing national service to block African guerrillas attempting to infiltrate from the north'.[4]

Some of the initial logistic difficulties in gaining access to Namibia were improved when SWAPO fighters were able (in the early 1970s) to pass through southern Angola into Ovamboland, Okavango and Kaokoveld. This route was not without its own problems, however as by this time UNITA was operating in southern Angola. UNITA was a rival nationalist organisation to SWAPO's ally, MPLA.

There is a close affinity between the Ovimbundu community in southern Angola, from which UNITA drew substantial support, and the Kwanyama community which straddles the Namibia/Angola border, many of whom were members of SWAPO or UNITA at that time. Together with the fact that both organisations were operating in the same area, this no doubt increased the likelihood of SWAPO and UNITA units interacting. This caused some problems between SWAPO and MPLA. There was, however, no alliance between SWAPO and UNITA as some have claimed.[5]

SWAPO itself knew that the armed struggle would be long and drawn out and (in 1971) stated:

> Many people ask themselves – and us – what is the point of a protracted guerrilla war like this one . . . However, what this war has done, is of great value to us: it has reinforced the spirit of unity in Namibia . . . Another result of our armed struggle is the insecurity it has created among the white population, in Namibia as well as in South Africa . . .
>
> The overall international attitude towards the Namibian question has changed considerably since 1966, when we launched our armed struggle . . . We do not mean that *only* the armed struggle has brought about a favourable attitude on an international level, many other factors are also involved. But it is the armed struggle, which means heavy losses and great sacrifices from our people, which is the crucial and convincing indicator of the entire Namibian people's unbreakable determination to be free.[6]

THE PORTUGUESE REVOLUTION AND ITS AFTERMATH

The Portuguese revolution of April 1974 was partly caused by pressure from the national liberation movements in Guinea-Bissau, Mozambique and Angola. It, in turn, led to the independence of these countries. This represented a major change in the balance of forces in Southern Africa and opened up a period of intense nationalist activity in the remaining white-ruled states of Namibia, Zimbabwe and South Africa. SWAPO summed up its significance as follows:

> We have seen a serious disruption taking place in the white colonial fort on African soil. The war against white minority rule will continue and we may still have a long way to go. However, we have seen that the situation may change overnight, in our favour, bringing our struggle and our victory forward.[7]

Equally important in boosting the morale of those who were fighting for freedom in Namibia and the rest of Southern Africa, was the victory of the FNL in Vietnam over the American forces that backed the regime in Saigon. This came in 1975 – only one year after the fall of the Caetano regime in Portugal. This defeat of a super-power by a national liberation movement was a source of great inspiration for other similar movements.

SWAPO's military wing was strengthened by having easier access to Namibia via Angola, and the improved lines of logistic support helped to transform its operations and eventually allowed SWAPO fighters to remain virtually permanently inside Namibia. The opening of the Angola border also meant that many more people were able to flee the repression of the South African regime, and many of those who did so reinforced SWAPO's military wing.

The intervention of South African troops in Angola on the side of UNITA and FNLA from August 1975, however, meant a general intensification of the war in the area both sides of the Namibia/Angola border, and involved SWAPO in regular clashes with FNLA and UNITA forces. This ultimately strengthened the alliance between SWAPO and MPLA.

From 1975 on there was a big increase in military operations in Namibia by SWAPO. The South African Defence Force itself admitted SWAPO's strength, political support and military skills:

> SWAPO sabotages electricity pylons, telephone poles, garages, industrial sites, bridges and other less important installations, by means of time bombs, land mines of Russian or other eastern bloc origin. The actions occur mainly in the operational area, the traditional white territory (Tsumeb, Grootfontein, Otjiwarongo triangle), but also in Windhoek, Swakopmund and Keetmanshoop.[8]

By 1979 the number of contacts between SWAPO and the South African Defence Force 'had doubled to an average of one a day while the total number of incidents increased from less than 500 in 1978 to over 900 in 1979'.[9] One of SWAPO's more spectacular successes was when it shot down a South African plane in southern Angola in March 1980, proving that it had acquired sophisticated weaponry, including anti-aircraft guns.[10]

SWAPO's ability to sustain and expand its armed struggle against South Africa rule has boosted its standing in the eyes of Namibians throughout the country. The impact of this on political developments should not be underestimated. It is a connection that has been made quite explicitly by SWAPO:

> Our colleagues are still using the [political] platform as their guns – which is of great importance ... we support them with arms. We are fighting in the bush and when they go on the platform they speak from a point of strength.[11]

THE MILITARISATION OF NAMIBIA

A significant indicator of the increase in SWAPO's guerrilla activity over the years is the rapid expansion of the size of the South African Defence Force deployed in Namibia. In June 1974 it was estimated that there were some 15,000 troops and counter-insurgency police in the country.[12] By September 1980 the number of troops alone (excluding police) was estimated at 70,000–80,000.[13] All this has been in defiance of the original League of Nations mandate that prohibited South Africa from establishing military bases in Namibia.

> A bewildering variety of military, paramilitary and police units are deployed in Namibia in defence of South Africa's illegal occupation ... Some of the forces ... operate in a deliberately low-profile, even clandestine manner ... The personnel ... include full-timers and part-timers; professionals, volunteers and conscripts; forces permanently based in Namibia, and forces based in South Africa but doing tours of duty in, or seconded to Namibia.[14]

The northern Bantustans are being used by South Africa as a buffer zone where they try to confine the war. Most of South Africa's troops are stationed in the north. The main bases are at Grootfontein, Ondangua, Rundu and Mpacha, with many other smaller bases throughout the region (see Map 9). Since this is a heavily populated area, the local people bear the brunt of the war. Nevertheless, the close relationship between SWAPO fighters and local people has not been undermined.

In a campaign to win the 'hearts and minds' of Namibians, South African soldiers have taken over the running of the schools, hospitals and other medical and public services in what they have designated the 'operational area'. In May 1979 this was expanded to cover half the country – placing it effectively under martial law. The police and army were given even wider 'powers of arrest, search and detention without charge or trial, and a number of restrictions could be imposed, such as curfews and bans on meetings'.[15]

From the early 1970s South Africa recruited black manpower into its armed forces. More recently, it has introduced 'ethnic units' whereby Namibians have been recruited and trained to fight against SWAPO. In August 1980 these units were integrated with a number of existing SADF units to form the South West Africa Territory Force (SWATF), and two months later conscription was extended to cover all Namibians. The effect of this measure was that, for the first time, Namibians were fighting against each other. The divisiveness of this policy is quite clear. The worst use of Namibians by the SADF is in Koevoet, a counter-insurgency unit which is notorious for its terror tactics, intimidation, assaults and murder employed against the civilian population.

A report by the Southern African Bishops' Conference in 1982 vividly described the state of militarisation in northern Namibia:

The Security Forces stop at nothing to force information out of people. They break into homes, beat up residents, shoot people, steal and kill cattle and often pillage stores and tea rooms. When the tracks of SWAPO guerrillas are discovered by the Security Forces the local people are in danger. Harsh measures are intensified. People are blindfolded, taken from their homes and left beaten up and even dead by the roadside. Women are often raped. It is not unknown for a detachment to enter a home and while black soldiers keep watch over the family, white soldiers select the best-looking girls and take them into the veld to rape them. There is no redress because reporting irregularities or atrocities to commanders is considered a dangerous or fruitless exercise . . . A dusk to dawn curfew is imposed in the operational area. Anybody moving after dark is shot. A person cannot even go to the help of a sick neighbour or woman in childbirth. A priest risks his life in going on a sick call . . . The whole complex of Security Forces in the operational area is designated by the (Ovambo) word omakakunya. We found it hard to determine the literal meaning of the word but its implications are by no means flattering – 'blood-suckers', 'bone-pickers' etc.[16]

In April 1987 South African forces burnt down 13 primary schools in northern Namibia.[17]

THE STRUCTURE OF SWAPO'S MILITARY WING

In the early 1970s a Military Council was set up by SWAPO

> to co-ordinate military activities and operations of the armed forces against the enemy ... To discuss and exchange past experiences, arising from both successes and set-backs encountered by the freedom fighters in the different parts of the country.[18]

The Council included the commander of SWAPO's military wing, political commissar, chief medical, logistics and intelligence officers and senior field commanders. It reported to the Secretary for Defence and Transport Peter Nanyemba, who in turn reported to the National Executive Committee and/or the SWAPO President, who is Commander-in-Chief.

The political commissar became an important figure, serving as a link between the National Executive and the military wing which, in the early 1970s, came to be known as the People's Liberation Army of Namibia (PLAN). This post carried with it the responsibility for 'communicating and clarifying party policy, party decisions and military strategy' and for the 'overall political development and morale of all SWAPO militants'.[19] SWAPO has made it plain that

> we don't divorce military from political matters – it is always politics which leads the gun. We have no purely military leaders; we are not militarists. Everybody in PLAN is politically motivated; our cadres are trained both politically and militarily, and the military is completely integrated into the overall structure of SWAPO.[20]

SWAPO fighters are permanently spread throughout Namibia, engaged in political mobilisation if not in military action, and there are areas of Namibia where South African administrative control has been completely undermined. The establishment of internal bases has been determined by military conditions within the country which favour roving guerrilla bases, not ones 'with aeroplanes, with tanks' like the SADF have.[21]

SWAPO's logistic supply centres are in Angola. These are run on a regular weekly schedule:

> We get up by six o'clock every morning. We go through our morning exercises, stop for tea and something to eat, then we go to our daily training, classes or duties ... On the weekends, we do washing and other tasks and

sometimes cultural things or sport like football. As in all guerrilla wars, however, the conditions are very tough . . . All of us must get used to them. So sacrifices are a necessary part of training in our camps.[22]

There is a division of labour, with specially trained units taking on the various tasks – medical, education, sports, repairs (of shoes, clothing, radios), etc. The medical and educational facilities are extremely important – the former for obvious reasons for any organisation engaged in an armed struggle. The educational work reflects SWAPO policy to try to overcome the disadvantages of the poor education system in Namibia. It is SWAPO policy to teach everyone to read and write in English (SWAPO has said it will adopt English as the official language of an independent Namibia so this is treated as a priority). Discussions and lectures are also organised by the political commissars.

Men and women receive the same training and work and fight side by side in mixed units in PLAN. There are also women commanders, although not without some problems at times. The fighters are ordinary members of SWAPO who volunteer to join PLAN. They are Namibians who feel they cannot any longer put up with conditions under South African rule. They leave their jobs, their villages, their schools, to seek better opportunities outside the country. Some are already committed to partaking in the armed struggle; others join in after they have left the country. As the number of recruits into PLAN has increased, more people, including some of those who had formed the early fighting units, were sent to study. Although not of all them have returned to PLAN, the level of education of SWAPO's fighters has gone up over the years. A major factor in this has also been the educational programmes within PLAN.

Some Namibians today feel that they are part of a direct line of resistance to colonial rule. They remember the stories of the wars fought by their parents and grandparents against the Germans and South Africans, and are inspired by them. Nevertheless, they acknowledge that Namibians failed to defeat the colonial powers in the past 'because they fought as a single tribe or single clan or single group'.[23] The lesson learned from Namibia's history is, therefore, that there must be a united involvement of all different communities and both men and women, to overcome South African rule. PLAN incorporates people from the various Namibian communities. The main bulk are, however, from northern Namibia where half the country's population lives, and where the war is most fiercely fought.

A number of alliances between nationalist organisations existed in Namibia in the early 1970s, but gradually they faded away as more and more groups and organisations joined SWAPO.

At the end of 1971 the National Convention (NC) was formed, bringing together the following: NUDO, led by Herero Chief Clemens Kapuuo; SWANU, headed by Gerson Veii; SWAPO, led by its Chairman David Meroro; the Volksparty of Rehoboth; the Voice of the People, a Nama/Damara group led by K. Conradie; the Namib African People's Organisation (NAPDO), a Damara organisation; DEMKOP; the Damara Tribal Executive; the Council of Nama Chiefs; and the Herero Chief's Council. Its aims were to bring the people of Namibia together 'in one National Unity', and fight for their 'total and complete' freedom and independence.[1]

The Chairman of the NC was Clemens Kapuuo. He had taken over as Herero Chief when Chief Hosea Kutako died, aged 100, in 1970. Kutako was mourned throughout Namibia and his life and work were commemorated internationally (there is a sculpture of him at the United Nations headquarters in New York). He had been a living link between the modern nationalist movement and the early resistance to colonial rule in Namibia. Kapuuo was a prominent teacher and nationalist figure and had acted as Kutako's deputy for many years. However his right to the chieftainship was disputed and a large group of Hereros opposed to his taking over as chief formed the Association for the Preservation of the Tjamuaha/Maharero Royal House, under the chairmanship of Revd B G Karuaera, a leader of the AME church in Namibia.

The first initiative of the NC was during Dr Waldheim's visit to Namibia in 1972. It did not embark upon any real political campaign within Namibia but it wanted to be regarded as the spokesman of the Namibian nationalist struggle. It therefore came into competition with SWAPO, which had already won considerable international recognition by this time. The internal wing of SWAPO had to deal with the other political groups in Namibia and naturally, therefore, participated in the NC. The work of the external wing, however, concentrated on the armed struggle and political lobbying in the international community, and it was with SWAPO's external leadership that the NC and its Chairman, Clemens Kapuuo, came into conflict. Matters got worse when the UN General Assembly voted in 1973 to recognise SWAPO as the 'authentic representative of the Namibian people'.[2] The NC eventually began to break up and SWAPO left it at the end of 1974, issuing a statement criticising Kapuuo, although he was not mentioned by name. This developed into a public row between Kapuuo and SWAPO. Kapuuo responded, in January 1975, condemning SWAPO and describing it as an Ovambo organisation that had no relevance to Namibians in central and southern parts of Namibia:

> The Ovambos who are today represented by SWAPO ... did not take part in the war against the Germans.
> SWAPO is ... an Ovambo political organisation because about 99 per cent of its members are Ovambos. When the Government of South Africa took over South West Africa ... [it] deprived the Africans of the central and southern parts ... of their lands, driving them to the desert and selling about 90 per cent of their lands to the White farmers who came from South Africa.
> The Government of South Africa did not deprive ... the Ovambos of their lands. They lived on their lands up to this day. For the tribes of the central and southern parts of South West Africa who have suffered terribly for more than 70 years under the German and the South African governments, their lands and their rights are very dear to them and cannot and will never allow their lands and their future to be decided by a political organisation of just one tribe which was not elected by them.[3]

The statement went on to call for the division of Namibia between north and south, along the border of the old German 'Police Zone'. This was a turning point in relations between Kapuuo and SWAPO. It was also a turning point in his relations with the South African authorities. Kapuuo had previously been in the forefront of the campaign against the South African regime. Eventually, however, he agreed to participate in the Turnhalle talks, which were organised by the South Africans on a purely ethnic basis. Three Herero members of SWAPO – Pejavi Muniaro, Godfrey Kumbee Tjizera and Otniel Kaakunga – responded with a letter attacking Kapuuo, after which Muniaro and Kaakunga were kidnapped and beaten up by Kapuuo's men.

In February 1975 the member organisations of the NC split in two directions – aligning either with SWAPO or with Kapuuo. Kapuuo insisted that as Chairman of the old NC he carried forward the old alliance, and renamed it the National Convention of Namibia (NCN). With him were the organisations he headed – NUDO and the Herero Chief's Council – the Liberation Party (a small Rehoboth group) and the Nama United Council. He later also claimed the support of three other small Nama/Damara groups – the South West Africa People's Democratic United Front (SWAPDUF), Damara United Front (DUF) and the Namibia Democratic Party.

The grouping around SWAPO reconstituted itself as the Namibia National Convention (NNC). It consisted of SWAPO, SWANU, the Volksparty, NAPDO, and the Damara Tribal Executive Committee. DEMKOP had by this time faded away, and its leader, Johannes Nangutuuala, worked for the Ovamboland Bantustan for a while. The NNC aimed to unite and 'educate and prepare the black population of Namibia politically and morally against the powers and structures that seek to destroy them'.[4] Its most useful function was, however, to create a collective voice for its various member organisations. Still, however, SWANU and some other groups had problems with SWAPO and accused SWAPO of not taking the alliance seriously. There was always some tension between SWAPO and SWANU, with SWAPO wanting to guard its own recognition and support and suspecting that SWANU was interested in unity to undermine that. It should also be remembered that these were the years of intense political activity by SWAPO and its Youth League within Namibia.

THE TURNHALLE TALKS

In 1974 South Africa announced that it would convene constitutional talks for Namibia. This was a device used by the South African regime to appear to meet the demands of the nationalist liberation movement and the international community, without actually giving up control of Namibia:

> The plan to stage a constitutional conference to discuss Namibia's fate was shaped by four major factors: the protracted tussle between the United Nations and the South African government over Namibia's future; Pretoria's overall policy in relation to the country and particularly its ethnic homelands or Bantustan programme; the

changing balance of forces in Southern Africa following the defeat of Portuguese colonialism in 1974, which compelled Vorster to seek a new *modus vivendi* in South Africa's relations with independent Africa; and the liberation struggle in Namibia itself, led by SWAPO.[5]

The talks eventually began on 1 September 1975 in the old German gymnasium or 'Turnhalle', by which name they came to be known. Most of those who participated were nominated by the South Africans. Political parties were excluded, and all 'representatives' were drawn on an ethnic basis, in accordance with the Odendaal Plan's proposals for Bantustans in Namibia (see Table 3). The participation of Chief Clemens Kapuuo was a major coup for the South African regime.

The NNC rejected the Turnhalle talks from the start, giving the following reasons:

(a) The talks are ethnically orientated and are aimed at furthering the Homeland system, and dividing the country on a racial line. Namibia's territorial integrity should at all costs be respected and maintained!
(b) The governments call them to attend the 'true leaders'. These . . . were not elected to go to the conference table. They were brought in as stooges to govern the homelands. How can they decide on the constitutional future of the country, if their constitutions in the homelands were sent to them from Pretoria?[6]

SWAPO called the talks a 'farce . . . aimed at the perpetuation of white minority rule under which South African domination would continue'.[7] It brought out its own constitutional discussion paper, prepared after consultations between the SWAPO leadership inside and outside the country. This called for a bill of rights, a directly elected legislature for a unitary state and an independent judiciary:

Our experience of persecution and racialism over many years has deepened our unqualified commitment to democratic rule, the eradication of racialism, the establishment of the rule of law and the entrenchment of human rights. Moreover, we reject absolutely any notion of Bantustans masquerading as federalism. SWAPO is pledged to the idea of a unitary state.[8]

The Turnhalle conference set up four special committees covering

Table 3   *Turnhalle Delegates on a Tour of Western Europe, 1975*

Name	Constituency/Position
Dr B J Africa*	Leader of the Rehoboth Council
P J Mouton*	Member of the Rehoboth Council
Geelbooi Kashe*	Ovakuruvehi (Bushmen)
Chief M Moraliswami*	Chief Councillor of the Caprivi Council
M Mamili	Caprivi Councillor for Justice and Community Affairs
A J F Kloppers*	Chairman of the Coloured Council
J J J Julius	Member of the Coloured Council
LJ Barnes	Member of the Coloured Council
E H L Christie	Leader of the Damara United Front (DUF)
J Skrywer	DUF member
J M Haraseb	DUF member
Chief Clemens Kapuuo	Herero Chief
J Karuaihe	Secretary to Kapuuo
E Tjingaete	Representing the Rietfontein Mbanderus
L Nganjone	Secretary to Tjingaete
A Majevero	Chief Minister of the Kavango Bantustan
S Kamwanga	Kavango Minister for the Interior and Justice
R Ngondo	Kavango Minister of Agriculture
D Luipert	Leader of the Nama delegation to the Turnhalle talks
E Kuhlmann	Member of the Nama delegation
W J Jagger	Member of the Nama delegation
Pastor Cornelius Ndjoba*	Chief Minister of the Ovamboland Bantustan
T Shiyagaya	Ovambo Minister of Works
F Indongo	Ovambo Minister of Economic Affairs
Revd P Kalangula	Member of the Ovamboland Legislative Council
S Mootseng	Tswana delegate to the Turnhalle talks
D F Mudge*	Senior Member of the White Executive Committee
E Van Zijl*	Member of the White Executive Committee
I Selebogo	Caprivian interpreter

Table 3 *continued*

Name	Constituency/Position
T P Bezuidenhout*	Official of the Ovamboland Bantustan
D E S Jacobs	Official of the Okavango Bantustan
D B Maytham	Official of the Caprivi Council
G H Marais	Secretary to the Turnhalle talks
J A Eksteen	Department of Foreign Affairs, Pretoria

Note *Participants in the Advisory Council of 1973
Source From the official list of Turnhalle delegates on a tour of Western Europe, West Germany, 26 October 1975.

1 discriminatory practices concerning wage scales, salaries, pensions, conditions of employment;

2 property rights in urban areas, economic infrastructure and finance;

3 social amenities, e.g. housing, public services, medical care; and

4 educational matters.

Decisions were arrived at by 'consensus', which obviously ruled out any vote by the black majority against the wishes of the white minority. The white delegation to the Turnhalle had no wish to see the sort of radical reforms needed to win the support of the overwhelming majority of Namibian blacks. It 'made use of the potential that exists for playing one tribal group off against each other, and . . . exerted an influence over conference proceedings out of all proportion to its size'.[9] Legal and technical advisers to the black delegations were encouraged, and were paid for by the South African regime,[10] and in the end the talks were inundated with 'experts' advising each ethnically based delegation. Other attempts to ensure the continued support of the black delegates included generous pay and allowances, hotel accommodation in Windhoek and general maintenance by the South African authorities.

The delegates were all sworn to secrecy about the conference proceedings. But some information leaked out, showing that there were heated debates about black and white sharing of amenities such as swimming pools and public libraries. There were also directly racist comments by some of the white delegates towards the black ones.

In January 1976 the UN Security Council, in Resolution 385, condemned South Africa for its continued illegal occupation of Namibia, demanded that it end its policy of Bantustans and homelands 'aimed at violating the national unity and the territorial integrity of Namibia' and declared that

> In order that the people of Namibia be enabled to freely determine their own future, it is imperative that free elections under the supervision and control of the United Nations be held for the whole of Namibia as one political integrity.[11]

A deadline of the end of August 1976 was set for South Africa to comply with this demand. On 18 August, the Turnhalle agreed to form an interim government, have full independence for Namibia by 31 December 1978 and maintain the country as a unitary state. It did not, however, speak of a South African withdrawal from the country.

It was not until March 1977 that the conference agreed on a 'Final Concept' – a Petition for the Establishment of an Interim Government. This laid out plans for a three-tier administrative structure in Namibia. At a national level was an elected National Assembly with members drawn from each ethnic group. One delegate from each group would also be on a Ministers' Council, headed by a President appointed by the South African state president. The representation in the National Assembly was to be as follows: Ovambos 12; Whites 6; Damaras 5; Hereros 5; Kavangos 5; Coloureds 5; Namas 5; Caprivians 5; Bushmen 4; Rehobothers 4; Tswanas 4. Pretoria was to retain powers over defence, external affairs, transport, finance and foreign exchange, internal security including the South African Defence Force and South African Police, post and telecommunications including broadcasting, and customs and excise, and sales policy.

The second-tier level was that of the ethnic group or Bantustan, termed 'representative authorities'. They were to have responsibility over all members of that particular ethnic group, with powers over land tenure, primary and secondary, but not tertiary, education, social welfare and housing, traditional administration of justice, amongst others. Any group not wishing to establish a representative authority would be looked after by the central government.

The third tier was that of the local or municipal authorities, with responsibility for managing urban areas, although this was still done on an ethnic basis and a black township such as Katutura was later designated as a different municipal area from Windhoek to avoid joint use of amenities by black and white.

This was merely the Odendaal Plan with allowance for a central authority elected on an ethnic basis. It has formed the basis of all South Africa's actions in Namibia since 1977, up to and including the Multi-Party Conference 'transitional government' installed in June 1985.

RESPONSES TO THE TURNHALLE PROPOSALS

The Turnhalle proposals did not receive any support from the international community and throughout 1976 and 1977 attempts were made by the UN to compel South Africa to adhere to UN resolutions over Namibia. These were blocked, however, by the Western members of the Security Council. In October 1976 France, the UK, and the USA vetoed for the third time UN efforts to take action, including economic sanctions, against South Africa for its refusal to withdraw from Namibia.

Within Namibia the Turnhalle proposals led to a political polarisation. The crucial question for all political groups became: Do we support or oppose the Turnhalle scheme? Those who opposed the scheme increasingly moved to join SWAPO.

In August 1976 the Rehoboth Volksparty disbanded to join SWAPO and in November the Namibia African People's Democratic Organisation (NAPDO) did the same. Even more significant, however, was the move to SWAPO in October 1976 of four communities representing some 80% of the 37,000 Nama people in southern Namibia. A statement outlining their strategy was signed by Pastor H Witbooi of Gibeon, grandson of Chief Hendrik Witbooi who led the Nama resistance to German rule in the 1904–7 war; J Stefanus of Vaalgras; S Isaks of Keetmanshoop; and H Noeteb of Hoachanas. It vividly portrays the mood of the times in Namibia and people's understanding of the South African Turnhalle strategy:

> In face of history and in face of our people we declare: We are on the eve of a time of political storms. The time of decisions has come ... But we can't speak from the ground, we need a platform to stand on ... Now there are only two platforms left: the national movement SWAPO or the Turnhalle. We asked ourselves: Who repressed, persecuted, humiliated, liquidated and betrayed us? Was

it SWAPO or the Boers and their allies? . . . Today we have arrived at this crossroad and our choice is clear: We join unconditionally in the genuine nationalist platform of SWAPO . . . the south of Namibia is politically lost to the South African government and its allies, the Turnhalle, as it is already in the centre and the north . . . Now we know that we waited too long for salvation from outside, first from the British, then from the Volkerebond [League of Nations] and finally from the UN. Now we will look ourselves for the new water. We will rely on our own forces.[12]

Then in April 1977 the Association for the Preservation of the Tjamuaha/Maharero Royal House, the Herero body that contested the leadership of Chief Clemens Kapuuo, and which had an estimated membership of 17,000, also disbanded to join SWAPO. This brought a broad section of the Herero community into SWAPO.

These moves were decisive in strengthening SWAPO's support throughout Namibia and helped to refocus attention on the nationalist campaign and away from the Turnhalle. This was the context of the UN General Assembly resolution of December 1976 that recognised SWAPO as the 'sole and authentic representative of the Namibian people' (my emphasis).[13] The General Assembly also decided that any independence talks should be with SWAPO, under UN auspices, for 'the sole purpose of discussing the modalities for the transfer of power to the people of Namibia'.[14] In other words, SWAPO was accepted as the principal actor in the effort to bring about national independence for Namibia.

With some of its members joining SWAPO, and SWAPO's increasing uneasiness at belonging to any alliance because of its own growing support, the Namibia National Convention ceased to function. In its place emerged the Namibia National Front (NNF) which consisted of those groups who did not join SWAPO but were still opposed to the Turnhalle. By 1977 the main NNF members were: the Damara Council, whose leader, Chief Justus Garoeb, was NNF President; SWANU, whose leader, Gerson Veii, was NNF Vice-President; the Mbanderu group of Hereros under Chief Munjuku Nguvauva; the National Independence Party (a Coloured group) under Charles Hartung; and the liberal white Federal Party under Bryan O'Linn.

The Turnhalle process even split the local wing of the Afrikaner National Party. Some of its members, headed by Dirk Mudge, who had been the party's deputy leader in Namibia, broke away to form the all-white Republican Party in late 1977. They supported the Turnhalle proposals and formed an alliance with the groups participating in the Turnhalle talks, which was called the Democratic Turnhalle Alliance (DTA). The rest of the Afrikaner National Party felt that the Turnhalle proposals went too far and they formed their own small alliance, AKTUR, claiming that they stood for the original Turnhalle principles but not its constitutional proposals. Two leading members of the National Party in Namibia, A H Du Plessis and Eben Van Zijl, headed this group and managed to get Hans Diergaardt, the leader of the Rehoboth Council, to join them.

The South African regime tried to win black support for the Turnhalle proposals by some limited reforms brought in towards the end of 1977. A new post of South African Administrator General in Namibia was created and filled by Justice M T Steyn from 1 September 1977. He introduced a number of measures that abolished the Mixed Marriages and Immorality Acts (forbidding marriage or sexual intercourse between black and white), and the pass laws that controlled Namibians' movement and where they might live. The Bantu Education system was also revoked, although the fundamental structure of education in Namibia remained unchanged and each ethnic group retained control of its own schools (and still does). In June 1978 a measure granting equal pay for equal labour was passed, although this had little effect as blacks and whites in Namibia rarely worked at the same level. In July 1978 trade unions were made legal.

However, South Africa also proclaimed the annexation of Walvis Bay (Namibia's only deep-water port) from 1 September 1977. Security regulation R17, imposed on northern Namibia after the 1971–2 strike, was lifted in November 1977, only to be replaced by new draconian security measures that extended the powers of the South African security forces to arrest and detain people without charge throughout the whole country. Nevertheless the South Africans claimed that they had done away with apartheid in Namibia.

Some Namibian nationalists began to return to Namibia from exile, believing that there was sufficient change for optimism about impending independence. Jariretundu Kozonguizi returned in 1976 and became legal adviser to the Herero delegation at the Turnhalle talks. He later joined the office of the Administrator General. Mburumba Kerina also returned in 1976 and worked for a German-funded foundation, PROSWA, which promoted the Turnhalle, although he went back to the

USA in 1978 after differences with his colleagues. Emil Appolus, a former SWAPO Secretary for Information and Publicity, returned in 1976 and worked as a journalist for a while before establishing himself as a businessman. SWANU's External Council was dissolved and its members returned to Namibia in 1977, where they worked within the NNF. They were joined in 1978 by Andreas Shipanga, former SWAPO Secretary for Information and Publicity and some other ex-SWAPO members, all of whom had been in detention in Tanzania.

In March 1978 DTA supporters provoked a fight with some SWAPO supporters in Katutura and Chief Kapuuo's bodyguard, Himuee Kambirongo, was killed. On 27 March Kapuuo himself was shot dead in the backyard of his shop in Katutura. In the days after the killing South African troop reinforcements were brought into Windhoek and Kapuuo's followers were armed by the South African regime, who immediately blamed SWAPO for the Chief's death. Serious fighting then broke out between Hereros and Ovambos (assumed to be SWAPO members), especially in Windhoek, and over 60 SWAPO members were arrested. SWAPO Executive Committee members, including the Deputy National Chairman, Daniel Tjongarero, received death threats and left the country. Some remained abroad but Tjongarero returned to Namibia. Kapuuo was buried at Okahandja, alongside his predecessor, Chief Kutako. He was succeeded by Kuaima Riruako, who became even more closely identified with the South Africans and their Turnhalle strategy than Kapuuo had been.

The fact that some people in SWAPO rejoiced at the death of Kapuuo was taken by the South African regime as 'evidence' that SWAPO had, indeed, killed him. But, as with the death of Chief Elifas in 1976, there were suspicions that the South Africans themselves might have been responsible. Even some members of Kapuuo's family now believe that he was killed by the South Africans.[15]

Throughout 1977–8 the western members of the UN Security Council negotiated with South Africa and SWAPO in an attempt to set aside the Turnhalle proposals and hold nationwide elections in Namibia under UN supervision and control. Nevertheless, South Africa went ahead with its original Turnhalle proposals and held ethnically based 'internal' elections in December 1978. They took place in an atmosphere of extreme intimidation and widespread propaganda promoting the DTA. SWAPO and the NNF boycotted the elections.

'Ruthless coercion' characterised both the registration of voters and the actual election.[16] South African troops monitored the polling and it was standard practice for polling officers to mark papers for voters. One report stated that 90 out of 100 voters had their papers marked for them.[17] In the light of these tactics the result was not surprising – 41 seats for the DTA out of a 50-seat constituent assembly. The constituent assembly and its successors have never, however, been recognised internationally or by the Namibian people.

16 THE DEVELOPMENT OF SWAPO

The demands and developments of the nationalist movement in Namibia transformed SWAPO from an organisation concentrating on straightforward political protest and petitioning, to a national liberation movement waging an armed struggle against the South African occupation regime, and engaged in social, educational and welfare programmes that were seen as a basis for the re-ordering of Namibian society after independence.

At the Second Annual General Conference of the Executive Committee, held in Dar es Salaam in 1965, various organisational problems were identified. Three issues figured strongly:

1 the lack of communication with SWAPO headquarters in Windhoek;
2 the need for improved budgetary and accounting procedures as the organisation increasingly received large sums from the OAU, the socialist countries, and support groups in the West; and
3 proper definition of the roles and responsibilities of leading officials and relations between them.[1]

With the launching of the armed struggle in 1966 were added new logistical and planning requirements but, apart from the training of men in the art of warfare. SWAPO's organisation and structure remained much the same as when it was formed at the beginning of the 1960s. There was a move, therefore, to reorganise and streamline SWAPO's structure, and a consultative congress was held at Tanga, Tanzania, for this purpose at the end of December 1969.

This was the first major gathering of SWAPO leaders and members abroad; the SWAPO leadership inside Namibia were not represented, as they were not able to travel outside Namibia. It was attended by about 30 people, including SWAPO's External Executive Committee, members drawn from the military wing, students, women and the representatives of

SWAPO's foreign missions. Also present were representatives from FRELIMO and the ANC of South Africa, and the Tanzanian Regional Commissioner, Mr Waziri Juma.

The conference made a number of amendments to SWAPO's constitution and changes in the leadership structure. The Vice-President, Louis Nelengani, was expelled for appearing as a state witness against Ja Toivo and others in the 1967–8 Terrorism Trial. Bredan Simbwaye, former President of CANU, was elected as the new Vice-President. Since Simbwaye was then in detention in Namibia, the former Vice-President of CANU, Mishake Muyongo, was elected as Acting Vice-President of SWAPO. The post of Secretary General was replaced by that of Administrative Secretary. Moses Garoeb was elected to that office. In 1984, Ja Toivo, just released from prison, was elected to the post of Secretary General.

A new National Executive Committee composed of ten elected and two appointed members, and a Central Committee of thirty elected members were also established, as were new departments to deal with different areas of responsibility, especially defence. Separate affiliated wings for women, youth and elders were also established.

The congress reaffirmed that 'armed struggle is the only effective way to bring about the liberation of Namibia.'[2] However it also emphasised the need for political mobilisation within Namibia and industrial action against the South African occupation regime. An attempt was made to improve communications between the leadership in Namibia and those in exile by specifying that those external leaders who had direct counterparts in Namibia in terms of the same functions and responsibilities were acting on behalf of those in the country.

THE SWAPO CRISIS OF 1976

In 1976 SWAPO faced a serious internal rebellion and a number of its members, including seven SWAPO Youth League leaders, the SWAPO Secretary of Labour, Solomon Mifima, and the Secretary for Information and Publicity, Andreas Shipanga, were arrested and held in detention by the Zambian authorities.

The origins of this rebellion go back to 1974, and the exodus of thousands of SWAPO members from Namibia after the collapse of the Portuguese empire and the floggings in Ovamboland. With the assistance of various international aid agencies, reception centres were set up by SWAPO to deal with the influx of refugees into Angola and Zambia and to meet their basic needs. However, the arrival of such a large group of people obviously presented SWAPO with real problems of providing food, accommodation, etc, and this led to some unrest.

Many of those who fled Namibia in 1974 were leaders and activists of the SWAPO Youth league (SYL). Some of these felt that they were not properly welcomed by the external leadership. Having played a leading role in SWAPO's political campaign in Namibia in the early 1970s they saw themselves as part of the overall SWAPO leadership and wanted to be treated as such. They began to demand that a congress (which was due) be held immediately, and openly criticised the external leadership, accusing them of incompetence and corruption, and calling for changes. SWAPO's internal inquiry into the rebellion stated that there was 'no power struggle in the top leadership of SWAPO, in the classical sense of the word ... However ... there was [a] power struggle waged by some elements in [the] SWAPO Youth League leadership against the mother body.'[3]

Andreas Shipanga and, to a lesser extent, Solomon Mifima, became associated with the SYL group and their demands for change. (Shipanga was also accused by SWAPO of making secret agreements with the West Germans and of being pro-Turnhalle.) Together they tried to mobilise support within SWAPO for change, aiming to secure key positions within the SWAPO leadership at the expected congress. The SWAPO leadership was convinced that 'the motive and ultimate aim of these dissidents was to seize power.'[4] Things came to a head, however, when a group of fighters in PLAN openly rebelled against the leadership.

For PLAN the arrival of large numbers of new recruits after 1974 meant extra demands on supplies of food, shelter, medicine, etc. and weapons and ammunition. This inevitably led to frustration among the fighters and some of the SYL group, keen to embark on military action against the South African regime, complained about shortages and inefficiencies. Towards the end of 1975 there was unrest at one particular base, Central Base, and this led 'to open revolt by cadres of Detachment "B" at the Eastern Front during the months of March-April, 1976'.[5]

The PLAN dissidents took control of SWAPO's Central Base. A team from the OAU Regional Office in Lusaka managed, however, to intervene and persuade them to come to Lusaka for talks with the SWAPO leadership. Here they were disarmed and detained. A group of about 50 other PLAN fighters set off for Lusaka to try to secure the release of their comrades. They were stopped by the Zambian army. A few are reported to have been killed; the rest were detained.

Shipanga and ten other SWAPO members, including seven SYL leaders and Solomon Mifima, who were considered to be the leaders of the rebellion, were detained on 21 April 1976.[6] They were held outside Lusaka, and then moved to Ukonga prison, in Dodoma, Tanzania, in mid-July 1976.

Many other SWAPO members who were thought to be involved in some way in the rebellion were detained at Mboroma camp, near Kabwe in Zambia. Newspaper reports from August 1976 through 1977 referred to 1,000 SWAPO fighters at Mboroma, although SWAPO denied that there were this many. The Mboroma camp was intended to be a rehabilitation centre. After some months a process of screening and reincorporation of those held there began. A small number chose to leave SWAPO and were given refugee status and care by the United Nations High Commissariat for Refugees (UNHCR). Nearly 600 were incorporated into the SWAPO health and education centre at Nyango, and by the end of 1977 the Mboroma camp had been dissolved.

In July 1976 South African armed forces attacked SWAPO camps at Sialola and Shatotua in western Zambia. The nature of the attacks made it clear that they knew the layout of the camps and their defences. This led SWAPO to believe that some of the PLAN fighters involved in the rebellion had co-operated with the South African army and given them information. Twenty-four people were killed and forty-five injured. SWAPO attributes this attack to Shipanga's followers and holds him responsible.

The SWAPO leadership set up an internal inquiry into the rebellion. It admitted 'official shortcomings and incompetence' as one of four factors that contributed to the rebellion, and came up with a number of recommendations to overcome them. The other factors were: enemy intrigues and infiltration; power struggle; and misguided elements.[7]

An international campaign to free Shipanga and the other dissidents in prison in Tanzania was launched, mostly by people who were generally supportive of the Namibian cause but who felt that SWAPO was harming itself by detaining people without trial. Representations were made to the Tanzanian authorities and to SWAPO, and although SWAPO did not take kindly to this campaign, the dissidents were released on 25 May 1978. They went first to various European countries that had agreed to offer them asylum.

Shipanga went at first to Sweden and on 23 June 1978 formed a new political organisation called SWAPO-Democrats (SWAPO-D), which he claimed was 'true to the original and traditional principles and policies of SWAPO'.[8] He went back to Namibia later in 1978, along with Mifima, Engombe, Moongo and Shikomba. SWAPO-D joined the Namibia National Front and for a while Shipanga was promoted as a nationalist leader with whom the South Africans might be prepared to settle. But it soon became apparent that he had no power base and SWAPO-D never really took off as an organisation.

THE 1976 NAMPUNDWE MEETING

In July 1976 SWAPO held an Enlarged Central Committee Meeting at Nampundwe, outside Lusaka in Zambia. This was the occasion to address the roots of the 1976 rebellion and make changes to improve the running of the organisation. The meeting also confirmed changes made at and following the Tanga congress, clarified and redefined the organisation's objectives, and adopted a new constitution and political programme. The division of responsibilities between departments was also clarified. The Departments of Defence and Transport were separated and the relations between the Department of Defence and PLAN strengthened, with the leading commander of PLAN reporting directly to the Secretary for Defence, Peter Nanyemba.

The Central Committee was introduced as the main decision-making body, with the Executive Committee its 'chief political bureau', putting into practice decisions of the congress and central committee, and formulating policy between the annual central committee meetings. The various wings – Youth, Women, Elders and PLAN – were made more accountable to the overall organisation, through the Central Committee on which they were all represented. PLAN was able to adopt its own rules, regulations and standing orders, and the other wings adopted their own constitutions, but these were all subject to the approval of the overall Central Committee.

In the new Political Programme, SWAPO made a firm commitment for the first time to the establishment of a future classless society in Namibia and pledged itself to

unite all Namibian people, particularly the working class, the peasantry and progressive intellectuals, into a

vanguard party capable of safeguarding national independence and of building a classless, non-exploitative
society based on the ideals and principles of scientific
socialism.[9]

This did not represent a sudden change in SWAPO's approach.
Rather, it must be seen in the context of developments in
southern Africa as a whole throughout the 1970s. The general
radicalisation of the subcontinent was a significant factor. Most
important, however, was the Namibian experience of South
Africa's continued refusal to withdraw from the country, the
inability of the UN to enforce its decisions on Namibia, and the
West's reluctance to support sanctions or other punitive
measures against South Africa. These factors came together
with SWAPO's growing concern to look to the future and
prepare for the reconstruction of the country after independence, and were also based on the experience of catering for
Namibians in exile in Zambia and Angola. Both in PLAN and in
its health and education centres in Angola and Zambia, where
most Namibians in exile live, SWAPO has created self-reliant
communities, where it tries to put into practice what it
preaches. The emphasis is on 'social justice and progress for
all'.[10]

SWAPO HEALTH AND EDUCATION CENTRES

The first such centre was established by SWAPO in the 1960s,
just outside Lusaka, at what came to be known as 'the old farm'.
This catered for a few hundred Namibians and provided the
basic medical and educational facilities – the latter consisting
of primary and adult education classes. By the end of 1974,
after the mass exodus of people from Namibia, this number had
risen to several thousand. A new site was then allocated to
SWAPO by the Zambian government, in the Western province
of the country. It was here that SWAPO set up the Nyango
Health and Education Centre. Later in the 1970s, more centres
were established in Angola. The main one, catering for over
70,000 Namibians, is now in Kwanza Sul, in central Angola.
    The centre at Nyango was built from scratch. By 1978 it was
home for over 5,000 Namibians, mainly women and children, a
'thriving community with schools, hospitals, fields of maize,
cabbages, potatoes, and workshops for electricity, carpentry
and sewing'.[11] There was a hospital run by the SWAPO

Deputy Secretary for Health and Social Welfare, Dr Libertine Amathila, and a staff of six:

> I am very proud of this hospital. We built it from nothing, bit by bit. This is so important for us. Even the crooked corridors give us pride, because this hospital was constructed by women who had never built a house before.[12]

Similarly, from a beginning in tents and corrugated iron shacks, the people at Nyango built their own accommodation and schools. Some of the buildings are prefabricated – donations to SWAPO from international aid agencies – but many others are made with local materials. Accommodation includes single and married quarters and large dormitories for the children. Vegetables, maize and beans are grown there and ducks and pigs are also kept.

Apart from adult literacy classes, the schools go from kindergarten to the Zambian Form 3 (third year of secondary school) and the syllabus used is the Zambian one. All the sixteen teachers and medical staff at Nyango are Namibian, an achievement in itself given the poor system of education provided by the South African regime in Namibia. They were, in fact, sent by SWAPO to study abroad and returned to teach at Nyango.

The main centre in Angola was first at Kassinga, 150 miles north of the Namibia/Angola border. But on 4 May 1978 the settlement was attacked by the South African armed forces in a combined air and ground attack:

> After the planes had fired rockets and dropped explosive and fragmentation bombs, as well as paralysing gases, the paratroopers landed on the terrain and during the six and a half hours that the attack lasted gave full vent to their basest instinct, indiscriminately massacring the terror-stricken population in cold blood.[13]

The casualty figures were: 612 Namibian refugees killed (147 men, 167 women and 298 children); 12 Angolan soldiers and 3 Angolan citizens killed; 611 Namibian refugees wounded; 63 Angolan soldiers and 15 Angolan civilians wounded.[14] The South Africans claimed that the settlement was a military base and that their attack was, therefore, justified. But foreign reporters who visited Kassinga reported that the dead in the mass graves were mostly women and children. Moreover, a South African Defence Force spokesman was later quoted as saying 'Many of our troops said afterwards that it was hell to have to shoot at women.'[15]

After the massacre at Kassinga, Namibians in exile in Angola were moved to Kwanza Sul province, where they established a new centre. Many people there lived at first in tents provided by aid agencies, although buildings were soon erected or adapted for the hospitals and and later for dwellings, schools, workplaces etc. Some 10,000 are of school age, with 7,000 below eight years old. Women and the elderly are other large groups.

As at Nyango, there is a complex of schools, library, kindergarten, etc. There are also further specialist training courses in practical and technical skills, such as nursing and other medical personnel, carpentry, typing, weaving, sewing. Two separate centres, one for small children and the other for practical training for women, have been established at Ndalatando, near the main settlement.

Once again, an effort is made to produce as much foodstuff as possible for the settlement's own needs and there are agricultural centres outside the main settlements. Water has been a particularly acute problem, however, as it had to be transported daily by truck from the nearest river. The lack of water and the sheer size of the settlement also made the spread of disease more likely. Much piped water is now laid on.

The communities are organised in a completely different way from traditional Namibian societies, and offer women especially considerable opportunities. Child-care is provided and those women who gain places and scholarships can study abroad. Within the centres themselves, women organise and manage the provision of social services, training programmes and food. There are also, however, training programmes specifically for women as administrators, accountants, radio broadcasters, communications officers, mechanics, electricians, etc.

Namibian women feel that they suffer 'three levels of injustice'.[16] First, as part of an oppressed nation; second from discrimination under the South African regime in Namibia; and third, from 'oppressive feudal practices which are still endemic in a large section of Namibian men'.[17] They believe that 'only within a socialist restructuring of society can women be liberated from the different forms of oppression and exploitation', and that in order to achieve that women will have to become 'active participants in the political, economic and administrative life of the society'.[18]

SWAPO is committed to women's equality but it still does not reflect this in its administrative structure. In 1982 there were only three women on the Central Committee – Dr Libertine

Amathila, Putuse Dwyili Appolus and Pendukeni Kaulinge – and none on the Executive Committee. (Putuse Appolus died suddenly in 1986.) Moreover, the very structure by which there is a separate Women's Council, although set up with good intentions, could lead to women's interests being marginalised.

Since the early 1960s, SWAPO and SWANU had both recognised the value of international lobbying in support of their cause. SWAPO, in particular, established a number of offices overseas, campaigned at the United Nations and maintained close links with the OAU and its Liberation Committee. SWAPO's external missions lobbied governments, national and international organisations, churches, trade unions and the press for support and understanding of their cause. Organising and raising funds for the defence of prisoners and detainees within Namibia was also a focal point of this work. By the mid-1970s

> SWAPO's quasi-diplomatic representatives at the UN and elsewhere were beginning to win increased humanitarian assistance in the West and more military assistance elsewhere. SWAPO was accepted by the OAU and the UN as the sole authentic representative of the Namibian people pending independence and elections ... It was allowed to participate in UN debates (but not to vote) on Namibian issues, and it was brought more closely into the work of the Council for Namibia. The UN General Assembly upheld the right of the Namibian people to seek, by whatever means necessary – including force – the liberation of their country.[19]

SWAPO has participated in meetings of various UN agencies, including UNESCO. It co-operated with the UN, and in particular with the UN Commissioner for Namibia, Séan McBride, in the setting up of the UN Institute for Namibia (UNIN) in Lusaka, which opened in 1976. UNIN was set up to carry out research, training, planning and related activities with special reference to the development of administrative staff and policy options for an independent Namibia. Its Director, Hage Geingob, is a member of SWAPO's Executive Committee.

SWAPO has also participated in the International Conferences on Humanitarian Law and on the Law of the Sea; in the

Non-Aligned Movement and in many national and international solidarity and non-governmental organisations. In 1975 the Commonwealth Heads of State Summit in Kingston, Jamaica, pledged financial assistance for the training of Namibians. This enabled Namibia, although not part of the Commonwealth, to benefit from this important grouping. Since then, SWAPO has expressed an interest in the possibility of Namibia joining the Commonwealth after independence, if the Namibian people so desire.

17 THE WESTERN CONTACT GROUP'S NEGOTIATIONS ON NAMIBIA 1977–8

The permanent Western members of the UN Security Council have consistently blocked any moves to compel South Africa to withdraw from Namibia. From 1970–6 Britain and the USA vetoed mandatory economic sanctions against South Africa three times, with France adding its veto on two of those occasions. One of the major reasons for this has been the continued economic investment from these and other Western countries in both Namibia and South Africa. These Western governments were anxious to protect such investment in the short-term. They also wanted to avoid a radicalisation of Southern Africa through a long-drawn-out armed liberation struggle, since this might jeopardise their long-term economic and strategic interests in the area. And they wanted to maintain some international credibility for their continued expressions of support for Namibian independence. Thus it was that in 1977 the five western members of the Security Council initiated negotiations with SWAPO and South Africa to try to reach a peaceful settlement in Namibia:

> We all felt that unity among the five would give us greater strength and lessen the chance of fragmentation of effort. We agreed to work with the frontline states to bring Nujoma and SWAPO into serious negotiations, taking care to have one or more frontline states present when the contact group met with SWAPO leaders. This would help to allay suspicion that we were trying to play the Africans off against each other. All contact group proposals were accordingly to be advanced jointly.[1]

In the first few months of 1977 representatives of what became known as the Contact Group of Western Nations held discussions with South Africa and the Front-line States. In early April they presented an aide-memoire to the South African Prime Minister B J Vorster, which outlined proposals for an independence settlement in Namibia that would be in line with UN Security Council Resolution 385. They added that an internal settlement based on the Turnhalle scheme was unacceptable to the international community and added a veiled threat of supporting sanctions against South Africa if it 'did not agree to early negotiations for Namibian independence'.[2] Vorster's initial reaction was to refuse to intervene in the Turnhalle process, but later in April he accepted the principle of elections in Namibia with some UN involvement. The essential points agreed were as follows:

1 elections would be held on the basis of universal suffrage for a constituent assembly whose task would be to decide upon a constitution for an independent Namibia;

2 the UN would be involved in the electoral process to ensure that they were free and fair. This 'might include a UN Special Representative appointed by the Secretary-General';[3]

3 the UN Special Representaive would ensure fair arrangements for the election and electoral process;

4 Namibians in exile would be free to return and participate in the electoral process;

5 the South African regime would, 'in consultation with those mainly involved', develop a plan for its withdrawal in stages from Namibia 'to prepare a smooth transfer of power at the end of the political process'.[4]

The release of detainees and political prisoners and the abolition of racially discriminatory legislation was left for a further date.

The Namibian churches, SWAPO's internal leadership and other political groups were briefed in Windhoek on 9 May by representatives of the Contact Group. SWAPO's Deputy National Chairman, Daniel Tjongarero, stressed that

> no atmosphere can be conducive for elections in Namibia, as long as the South African armed forces, police and administration is still in Namibia ... we should also stress that no elections can be fair as long as there is no UN supervision and control of such elections, and we stress 'control'.[5]

Anxious that SWAPO's internal leadership should not be played off against the leadership abroad, Tjongarero stressed that

> SWAPO is geographically divided, but there are not two SWAPOs, as many want to believe. Any response to the [Contact Group's] report should and would come from the whole SWAPO.[6]

On 15 May 1977 the Contact Group representatives briefed SWAPO leaders in Maputo, Mozambique. In response, SWAPO raised a number of substantial issues and questioned the proposals and their wording. The main points were:

1 that the withdrawal of the South African administration and armed forces, and the unconditional release of all Namibian political prisoners were crucial to the electoral process;

2 that a settlement must not only be 'internationally acceptable' but also acceptable to the Namibian people;

3 which Namibians groups would be involved in the negotiations (here SWAPO recalled its recognition by the UN General Assembly as the 'sole and authentic' representative of the Namibian people);

4 the time limit set for negotiations;

5 the nature of South Africa's intended interim central administrative authority and its powers;

6 the nature of UN involvement in the electoral process (here the importance of UN *supervision* and *control* as spelled out in UN Security Council resolution 385 was stressed); and

7 the means of transferring power and arranging a South African withdrawal from Namibia.[7]

The question of control of the electoral process became a major issue in the negotiations. Moreover, it was clear that South Africa intended to go ahead with the Turnhalle scheme and wanted this to be the basis of an interim authority in 'control' of Namibia during the electoral process. Cyrus Vance reported that 'despite what Vorster told the Contact Group, the South Africans intended to follow a two-track strategy: preparing the option of an internal settlement, while at the same time continuing to explore the possibilities for a wider solution.'[8]

The South Africans also refused to commit themselves on the size and nature of the UN military and administrative presence during elections. The Contact Group therefore 'began a detailed study of the functions the UN might perform in the transition period, looking particularly at ways to monitor effectively the political process leading up to UN supervised elections'.[9] Initially, the Contact Group mentioned a possible UN monitoring group of only 1,000.[10] SWAPO countered by suggesting 3,500 – 4,000.[11]

When South Africa appointed its first Administrator General in Namibia, Justice M T Steyn, who took up the post on 1 September 1977, the question of control became focused on who would have superior authority during the electoral process – the South African Administrator General or the proposed UN Special Representative. The Contact Group stressed that the Special Representative would have the responsibility of satisfying himself that:

- the existing legislation is non-discriminatory and does not impede the full participation of all Namibians in the political process;
- the proposed electoral legislation is adequate;
- the political campaign is fairly and peacefully conducted . . .
- the registration of voters is properly and comprehensively carried out;
- voting is secret and free from improper interference by anyone;
- the votes are properly counted and the results are properly declared.[12]

There was also early disagreement over the question of the withdrawal of South African troops. South Africa agreed to a withdrawal 'by independence, subject to the views of the new government'.[13] SWAPO wanted a complete withdrawal within three months of a ceasefire and before political campaigning began for the elections. SWAPO also stressed that the UN monitoring group should include an armed peace-keeping force. The Contact Group felt it unlikely that the South Africans would agree to withdraw all their troops before an election and 'expressed the view that the duties envisaged by SWAPO for a UN peace-keeping force could effectively be carried out by either civilian or military observers'.[14]

Another dispute arose over the issue of political prisoners and the qualification for that status. The Contact Group suggested an international panel of jurists, which would include two South Africans. SWAPO wanted the legal section of the staff of the UN Special Representative to decide any disputes. The South African regime acknowledged for the first time that it was holding Namibian political prisoners, but accused SWAPO of having some too – referring to Andreas Shipanga and others who were then in prison in Tanzania. President Nyerere's decision to release the Shipanga group in May 1978 was no doubt influenced by wider political considerations such as this.

South Africa insisted early on that Walvis Bay should not be included in the negotiations, and asserted that it was part of South Africa, not Namibia. Then on 1 September 1977 South Africa proclaimed that the port would be administered as part of the Cape Province. Their claim rests on the colonial treaty of 1878 by which Britain annexed the enclave of Walvis Bay to prevent its falling into the hands of the Germans. It is Namibia's only deep-water port and is of crucial importance to the economic growth of a future independent Namibia, as well as being strategically significant to South Africa's and the West's control of the Cape route. Since the League of Nations mandate, however, the port has been administered as part of Namibia. All Namibian nationalist organisations have claimed that Walvis Bay is historically, culturally, geographically and economically an integral part of Namibia and do not envisage leaving the area under continued South African control. But the Contact Group were aware that 'if the independence negotiations had to resolve the status of Walvis Bay, on which the sides were diametrically and immovably opposed',[15] their initiative would be destroyed.

After further talks and consultations the Contact Group put forward the following revised proposals in October 1977:

1 a South African force of 1,500 men would remain in Namibia, confined to one base, under UN monitoring, until independence;

2 all political prisoners would be released;

3 the UN monitoring team would include a military peace-keeping force of about 2,000, the exact number still to be determined;

4 measures would be taken to neutralise the South African police and militia in Namibia;

5 the status of Walvis Bay would be deferred for negotiation after independence.[16]

Both South Africa and SWAPO rejected these proposals. To try to break the deadlock, 'proximity talks' were held in New York in February 1978. The SWAPO delegation included leaders based in Windhoek and those in exile. The South African delegation included, for the first time, representatives from the Turnhalle. SWAPO accepted that 1,500 South African troops remain in Namibia through the elections. Pretoria's response to this came when South African Foreign Minister R F Botha walked out of the talks altogether.

Further amendments were then made to the proposals as follows:

1 The South African-appointed Administrator General would retain control of the Namibian police, who would be accompanied in their duties by UN observers;

2 The UN Special Representative would determine the size of the monitoring group and peace-keeping force . . .

South Africa would be consulted on the national composition of the UN force to ensure that it was not drawn primarily from nations avowedly sympathetic to SWAPO;

3 The Contact Group would take into account the wishes of the constituent assembly chosen during the UN-supervised elections if it asked that the South African forces remain in Namibia after the elections; and

4 South African forces could be concentrated at two bases in northern Namibia.[17]

On 10 April 1978 these final proposals were presented to the UN Security Council. On 25 April South Africa formally accepted the proposals 'in principle'.

A mere nine days later, on 4 May 1978, South African forces attacked the Namibian refugee settlement at Kassinga, 150 miles inside Angola. SWAPO President Sam Nujoma was in New York at the time of the Kassinga attack, in talks with the Contact Group. He immediately returned to Angola and the whole future of the Western initiative was in doubt. Cyrus Vance reported that

the larger question on my mind was whether South Africa was sincere about trying to negotiate an acceptable settlement. Given the size of the attack and the prior intelligence work and military planning it required, it seemed that Pretoria must have been preparing the raid even as Vorster was agreeing to our clarified proposal.[18]

The Contact Group's proposal specified a three-month period for the withdrawal of South African troops and then a four-month election campaign, so the initial ceasefire would need to come into force in May 1978 at the latest to allow independence by 31 December 1978 – the date set by the Turnhalle and South Africa and accepted by the Contact Group. The attack on Kassinga therefore seems clearly to have been an attempt by South Africa to get SWAPO to reject the proposals or delay in responding to them.

Despite the Kassinga attack, however, SWAPO agreed to the Contact Group's proposal on 12 July 1978, on condition that they support a proposed UN Security Council resolution affirming that Walvis Bay was an integral part of Namibia. The South Africans were 'extremely upset' at this.[19] Nevertheless, on 27 July the Security Council adopted two resolutions on Namibia. Resolution 431 took note of the Contact Group's proposals; requested the Secretary General to appoint a Special Representative for Namibia 'in order to ensure the early independence of Namibia through free elections under the supervision and control of the United Nations'; and urged the Secretary General to submit recommendations for the implementation of the proposal 'in accordance with Security Council resolution 385 (1976)'.[20] Resolution 432 declared that 'the territorial integrity and unity of Namibia must be assured through the reintegration of Walvis Bay' and gave its full support to 'the initiative of steps necessary to ensure the early reintegration of Walvis Bay into Namibia'.[21]

18 THE UN PLAN FOR
INDEPENDENCE ELECTIONS IN NAMIBIA

UN Security Council Resolution 431 meant, in effect, that the UN had taken up the Contact Group's proposals and, from July 1978 on, the UN prepared detailed measures for their actual implementation. The Contact Group still played a role in the continuing negotiating process, however.

The UN Commissioner for Namibia, Martti Ahtisaari, relinquished his post and was appointed as Special Representative on Namibia to the UN Secretary General. In early August 1978 he went to Namibia to assess the practical requirements of the UN monitoring group. On the basis of Ahtisaari's findings, the UN Secretary General gave a report to the Security Council.[1]

This report recommended a UN Transitional Assistance Group (UNTAG) consisting of a civilian component of 1,860 and a military one of 7,500. Both figures were substantially higher than either SWAPO or South Africa had envisaged. The civilian component was to assist the Special Representative in ensuring that the elections were free and fair and to cover the proposed 400 polling stations. The military component was to:

1 monitor the ceasefire, the restriction of South African and SWAPO troops to base, the phased withdrawal of all but 1,500 South African troops and the restriction of those 1,500 to specified locations;

2 prevent the infiltration of Namibia's borders;

3 monitor the demobilisation of citizen forces, commandos and ethnic forces and the dismantling of their command structure.

The report noted that South Africa still wanted to hold elections in December 1978 and wished, therefore, to shorten the transitional period to fit in with this, but it left the final date of independence up to the elected constituent assembly. The transitional period was to start on the date of approval of his report by the Security Council, and the elections to take place seven months later. As no specific period of time had been suggested for the elected constituent assembly to adopt a constitution and move towards formal independence, the report envisaged that UNTAG would be in place for about one year in all.

SWAPO welcomed the Secretary General's report. It had some outstanding reservations about certain details, but proposed nevertheless that it sign a formal ceasefire with South Africa to initiate the transitional period.[2]

South Africa's response was angrily to claim that the report deviated from the Contact Group's proposals.[3] They insisted on independence by 31 December 1978 and the shortening of the time-table for the transitional electoral period to four months to fit in with this. They also strongly objected to the size of the military component of UNTAG. The South African Foreign Minister, R F Botha, complained that the South African government had accepted the Contact Group's proposals, 'nothing more, nothing less,' and said 'We are prepared to adhere to that decision but not to go along with interpretations inconsistent with the proposal.'[4]

Then on 20 September 1978 the South African Prime Minister, B J Vorster, announced his resignation. At the same time, he formally rejected the UN Secretary General's report on implementation of the Contact Group's proposals, and announced that South Africa would go ahead with internal elections in Namibia in December 1978 'in order to establish unequivocally who had the right to speak for the people of South West Africa'.[5]

On 29 September the UN Security Council approved the Secretary General's report in Resolution 435. This became known as the 'UN Plan'. In view of South Africa's stand, however, its implementation was immediately in question.

In a final effort to rescue the proposals for independence elections under UN supervision and control, the Contact Group Foreign Ministers flew to Windhoek and Pretoria in mid-October 1978 to meet the new South African Prime Minister, P W Botha.[6] Although they hoped to be able to persuade Botha to drop the proposed internal elections in Namibia, they did not succeed. The British Foreign Minister, Dr David Owen, has stated that

> There was no way that we could stop Pieter Botha . . . he was going ahead with this internal settlement. Therefore the only thing we could salvage was an agreement that he would not rule out UN elections and that the internal elections would be done by him and would have no relevance.[7]

It was agreed that South Africa go ahead with internal elections in Namibia and that it would persuade the constituent assembly then elected to agree to the UN plan. This was in direct conflict with the Contact Group's original proposals which had been endorsed by the UN Security Council.

This agreement can only be described as a humiliating defeat for Western diplomacy, and, more importantly, it was a major setback for the UN's attempt to settle the problem through negotiation. Although the West had stated that it would not recognise the elections, the agreement allowed South Africa further to promote Turnhalle members as 'elected' leaders. South Africa still had not given any undertaking to implement the UN election plan and it became clear that even in the face of open defiance, the West was unwilling to impose sanctions against South Africa.[8]

SWAPO and the African states at the UN rejected this agreement and on 13 November the UN Security Council condemned South Africa's decision to go ahead with internal elections.[9] The Contact Group abstained and Cyrus Vance reported that 'Western credibility with the African states was damaged by this vote.'[10]

DEVELOPMENTS SINCE 1978

The internal elections were held in Namibia in December 1978, amidst widespread fraud and intimidation of voters. The Democratic Turnhalle Alliance (DTA) claimed victory and gained control of a newly established constituent assembly, although this had no real power.

After the internal elections there were repeated attempts by the Contact Group and the UN to implement the UN plan, but South Africa constantly introduced new issues or problems to be resolved. In January 1979 the UN Special Representative, Martti Ahtisaari, visited Namibia with the Indian Commander of UNTAG's military component, Lt-General Prem Chand, to complete consultations on the requirements for the deployment of UNTAG. In February 1979 the UN Secretary General sent ceasefire letters to be signed by SWAPO and South Africa, intended to initiate implementation of the UN plan. The ceasefire was scheduled to start on 15 March 1979, but the South Africans objected to the arrangements for monitoring SWAPO fighters and the composition of the UNTAG military contingent.[11] The ceasefire letters were never signed. In fact, both SWAPO and South Africa requested that the UNTAG military component be made up of troops from countries which were friendly, or at least not hostile, to them.[12]

The question of where SWAPO fighters were to be confined to base had by this time become a major issue. SWAPO stated that its '2,500 guerrilla forces' should be confined to bases inside Namibia:

> [The] SWAPO guerrilla army, being mobile, has no permanently structured bases. Therefore, for the purpose of implementing the UN Plan, it has been agreed upon during the negotiations between SWAPO and the Five that specific bases will have to be identified to which SWAPO armed forces would be confined . . . SWAPO will provide military liaison officers in order to ensure effective coordination and consultation with the military component of UNTAG.[13]

South Africa refused to accept that SWAPO had fighters permanently inside Namibia who could be confined to bases within the country. They also feared that any SWAPO fighters outside Namibia would cross into the country during the electoral process. The UN and the Contact Group, therefore, proposed the creation of a demilitarised zone along the Namibia/Angola border. Discussions over this were drawn out over many months.

Then in January 1981 the UN brought both sides together in a 'Pre-Implementation Meeting' in Geneva, to try to resolve all outstanding issues. Delegations came from SWAPO, South Africa and the DTA, with South Africa trying to use the meeting to promote the DTA and encourage direct talks between it and SWAPO, thus 'Namibianising' the issue. South Africa and the DTA also accused the UN of bias in favour of SWAPO. Then, in the middle of the meeting, South Africa announced that it was 'premature to proceed with the discussion of the setting of a date for implementation',[14] and the talks broke up.

In March 1981 the UN General Assembly held a Special Session on Namibia which adopted ten resolutions condemning South Africa and calling on the Security Council to impose comprehensive sanctions. The Contact Group countries abstained on all these resolutions. Then in April they vetoed four Security Council resolutions calling for sanctions against South Africa and for an oil embargo and measures to strengthen the arms embargo.[15]

THE US ELECTION FACTOR

A key factor in the South African withdrawal at Geneva was the victory of the Republican Ronald Reagan in the US Presidential election. He came into office in January 1981, making it quite clear that he would change US policy towards South Africa, and that he favoured 'constructive engagement', under which direct pressure on South Africa for change would not be considered. Reagan soon asserted his leadership of the Contact Group and took over control of the pace and content of the West's policy towards Namibia. The US administration then introduced new issues to be resolved before the UN plan could be implemented. These were proposed 'constitutional principles' to be agreed in advance of meetings of the constituent assembly which was to be formed after UN elections, and the linkage of Namibian independence to the withdrawal of Cuban troops from Angola.

The idea of constitutional principles was influenced by the Lancaster House agreement on Zimbabwe: they were designed to reassure white settlers in Namibia and the whites in South Africa itself. They were drawn up by the Contact Group after discussions between the US and South African governments and included a Bill of Rights, independent judiciary, the protection of private property, and no introduction of criminal offences with retrospective effect.[16] SWAPO accepted these principles but would not accept proposals for a confusing two-vote system combining proportional representation and a single-member constituency system.

The linkage of Namibian independence with the situation in Angola had, however, much more serious implications. It showed that the US administration viewed Africa as a theatre for East-West conflict rather than as a continent with its own dynamics. It also offered the South Africans an excuse for not proceeding with the implementation of the UN plan. The Cuban troops remain in Angola to protect that country from attacks by South African armed forces and the rebel movement UNITA, which South Africa supports and arms. Thus the withdrawal of the Cubans from Angola could be brought about by a change of policy by South Africa. Yet South Africa still says it cannot proceed with Namibian independence until Angola is free of the Cubans.

SWAPO and the front-line states have consistently refused to accept the concept of linkage between the decolonisation of Namibia and the question of Cuban troops in Angola. The

British, West German, Canadian and French governments have all said that they do not believe that the withdrawal of Cuban troops from Angola should be a precondition for Namibian independence. France, in fact, under the Socialist administration elected in 1981, temporarily suspended its participation in the Contact Group in 1983, over the linkage issue.[17] Other Contact Group members, however, made little effort to overcome this issue. The British Prime Minister, Mrs Margaret Thatcher, aptly summed up the problem when she pointed out that 'the fact that other nations have made the linkage is material to how and when the problem will be resolved.'[18] The question of Namibian independence is thus no longer a straightforward issue of self-determination, but has been made part of wider political and strategic concerns.

In 1983 the DTA administration in Namibia collapsed, due to its failure to initiate substantive reforms or win local or international support, and due to financial mismanagement. In June 1985 South Africa established an 'interim government' in Namibia which consisted of the DTA plus a few small black political groupings. It has remained deadlocked over the question of constitutional reform. South Africa still insists on retaining the ethnic division of Namibia. Nevertheless, it maintains that it is keeping the door open for an internationally acceptable independence solution. The international community, meanwhile, is still seeking ways of implementing UN Security Council Resolution 435.

CONCLUSION

Only just over 100 years ago the various societies in Namibia were still independent, although European missionaries, traders and settlers were already encroaching on their land and culture. None of these societies willingly or passively accepted foreign rule. At the same time, however, none was able to resist the imposition of that rule at all times. Nor were they ultimately able to stop the consolidation of German, and later South African, control. In the final analysis, as in so many other parts of Africa, those with superior weaponry had the upper hand.

Nevertheless, although they separately resisted the imposition of foreign rule, there was a clear attempt by Namibian societies in the centre and south of the country to form a united front against the German colonial regime. Unity was not then achieved; the Namibian resistance was overcome by the Germans. But unity was already perceived as necessary for a successful resistance to foreign domination.

Throughout the 1920s various communities resisted the full imposition of South African rule, again without success, however. Then new forms of organisation began to spring up – cultural associations, educational organisations, independent churches, and labour organisations. Some of the traditional community leaders, such as Herero Chief Hosea Kutako and his Chief's Council, took a consistent stand against South African rule, and petitioned the United Nations for an end to South African rule, but others were incorporated into the new administrative structures and no longer truly represented their peoples' interests.

It was from the centres of traditional resistance and the new forms of organisation that the move towards specifically nationalist objectives took place in 1958–60. OPO, which represented the contract workers from the north, specified the attainment of independence in its constitution. The first organisation set up specifically to work towards self-determination of the Namibian people was SWANU, which was intended as an umbrella organisation in which various anti-South African groups could act jointly. Then OPO changed its name – to SWAPO – and its status, becoming also an overtly nationalist organisation.

Initially, both SWANU and SWAPO saw a key role for the United Nations in Namibia's path to independence, with a possible period of UN trusteeship for the country. But the early 1960s saw a change away from this position, towards the desire for full independence straight away. At the same time there was a shift away from reliance on petitioning the UN as a means of achieving independence. A major contributory factor in this was the failure of the UN to enforce its own decisions on Namibia and, more specifically, the refusal of the ICJ in 1966 to judge South Africa's administration of the country. A new form of resistance was then called for. This was the context for SWAPO's decision to embark upon an armed struggle against South African rule. SWANU approved in theory of the need to take up arms, but was not prepared itself to do so.

The increasing support for SWAPO within Namibia and in international forums was in part because of this decision to take up arms. It was, however, also related to its original base amongst the contract workers, as well as to the way SWAPO worked with established anti-South African groups in the country, in particular, the Herero Chief's Council. SWANU, on the other hand came into conflict with the Chief's Council and did not manage to widen its support-base beyond the incipient intelligentsia.

Throughout the 1960s and 1970s Namibian nationalists were active in opposition to South African rule and South Africa's plans to divide the country on an ethnic basis into Bantustans. By the end of the 1970s, SWAPO had emerged as the major nationalist organisation in the country. The widespread support it received from groups in the centre and south of Namibia who joined SWAPO in 1976–7 helped to make it a truly national movement.

After 1975, an independent Angola provided SWAPO's military wing, PLAN, with wider access to Namibia and with improved lines of communications SWAPO was able to expand and develop its armed struggle against the South African occupation regime in Namibia. PLAN units began to operate throughout the northern region, and reached places such as Tsumeb and beyond. Some units now live on a semi-permanent basis within the country and are part and parcel of the local communities. The war is, nevertheless, still mostly confined to northern Namibia – the northern Bantustans and the Kao-koveld, providing natural barriers to PLAN's penetration of South African controlled farming and industrial areas. But it takes some 80,000–100,000 South African military and parami-litary forces to avert a SWAPO military victory.

The internal crisis SWAPO experienced in 1976 is not without its parallels elsewhere in Africa in the history of other nationalist movements. What is interesting, though, is SWAPO's readiness, in this instance, to countenance a Commission of Enquiry, whose findings and recommendations showed up many problems in SWAPO's organisational procedures and leadership, and a readiness to try to overcome these.

The challenge of a long drawn-out nationalist campaign and a decade of armed struggle, together with the problems created by the needs of thousands of Namibians in SWAPO's care and by the internal crisis, compelled SWAPO to redefine its objectives at its 1976 Enlarged Central Committee Meeting. Here SWAPO adopted a new Constitution and Political Programme. Through the latter, SWAPO dealt with the type of society it envisaged after independence. It chose a socialist path of development, reflecting the general radicalisation of the national liberation movements in southern Africa in the face of the intransigence of the ruling white minority regimes.

SWAPO has succeeded in challenging the South African illegal occupation regime in Namibia through its politcal mobilisation within the country, as well as through its armed struggle. It has also organised thousands of Namibian refugees in Zambia and Angola into increasingly self-reliant communities, and has achieved considerable international standing and support.

The UN has not been able to establish its authority over Namibia since the termination of the mandate because it was blocked from taking action against South Africa by Western vetoes in the UN Security Council. Thus, despite the moral and legal legitimacy accorded to the cause of Namibian nationalists by the country's unique international status, the UN has not succeeded in bringing the country to independence.

The current deadlock over negotiations to implement the UN plan for fair and free elections in Namibia under UN supervision and control has been caused by the linking of Namibian independence to the internal situation in Angola.

The question of Namibian independence is seen not as a straightforward issue of self-determination but as part of wider political and strategic concerns. Under such conditions, prospects for a negotiated settlement of Namibian independence receded.

At the same time, the internal situation in South Africa is of importance to Namibia's future. There are some who argue that the regime in Pretoria is unlikely to accept Namibian independence in the face of the threat of a widespread black uprising in

South Africa, because it fears a possible white backlash and encouragement to black South Africans if it did so. Others argue that Namibia will be used by the South African regime as a card or pawn to play as it tries to hold off sanctions and other international pressure for change within South Africa itself.

Certainly, the South African regime has yet to be convinced that the advantages of a Namibian settlement would outweigh what it perceives as the risks involved. This is not to say that Namibia's independence rests solely on changes within South Africa. It depends on a combination of forces coming together at the same time: negotiations, political and economic pressure and the armed struggle.

There will come a time when South Africa judges that it is more advantageous for it to withdraw from Namibia. The combined pressure of political and military resistance to the South African regime both in Namibia and in South Africa itself will play a major role here. But also important will be the reaction of Western governments to South Africa's continuing efforts to control and, at times, destabilise the whole of southern Africa, and their reactions to the continuing nationalist campaign in Namibia and South Africa. If Western governments feel that their interests in southern Africa can no longer be protected by the South African regime they may choose to step in. In the meantime their inaction protects the South African regime and helps to perpetuate its illegal occupation of Namibia.

NOTES

Chapter 1

1 Cited in Brigitte Lau, 'The Emergence of Kommando Politics in Namaland, Southern Namibia 1800–1870', MA thesis, University of Cape Town, 1982, p 38.
2 Ibid, p 38.
3 Ibid, p 36.
4 Richard Moorsom, 'Colonisation and Proletarianisation: An Exploratory Investigation of the Formation of the Working Class in Namibia under German and South African Colonial Rule to 1945', MA thesis, University of Sussex, 1973, p 15.
5 See Lau, 'Kommando Politics in Namaland'.
6 W G Clarence-Smith, 'The Angolan Connection in Namibian History', International Conference on Namibia 1884–1984, London, September 1984, p 2
7 Ibid.
8 H Vedder, *South West Africa in Early Times* (Oxford, Oxford University Press, 1938), p 7. See also Moses Garoeb, 'African Resistance: The Early Days', paper presented to the Namibia International Conference, Brussels, May 1972.
9 Lukas de Vries, *Mission and Colonialism in Namibia* (Johannesburg, Ravan Press, 1978), p 73.

Chapter 2

1 I Goldblatt, *History of South West Africa: From the Beginning of the Nineteenth Century* (Cape Town, Juta and Co, 1971), p 133.
2 Cited in H Drechsler, *'Let Us Die Fighting'. The Struggle of the Herero and Nama against German Imperialism 1884–1915* (London, Zed Press, 1980), p 143.
3 H Bley, *South West Africa Under German Rule* (London, Heinemann, 1971), p 149.
4 Ibid, pp 163–4.
5 Ibid, p 150.
6 Cited in Drechsler, *'Let Us Die Fighting'*, p 201.
7 Bley, *SWA Under German Rule*, p 150.
8 Ibid, p 151.
9 Michael Scott, 'Record of a meeting with Frederick Maharero, Paramount Chief and other representatives of the Herero people at present in exile in Bechuanaland. The meeting took place at Mafeking on July 14th, 1947', in 'Southwest Africans Appeal to the United Nations', AB48/5 Rhodes House, Oxford.
10 SWAPO, *To Be Born A Nation. The Liberation Struggle for Namibia* (London, Zed Press, 1981), p 19.

Chapter 3

1 Cited in R W Imishue, *South West Africa: An International Problem* (London, Pall Mall Press, 1965), p 67.
2 Robert Leroy Bradford, 'Blacks to the Wall', in Ronald Segal and Ruth First (eds) *South West Africa: Travesty of Trust* (London, Andre Deutsch, 1967), p 93.
3 Ruth First, *South West Africa* (Harmondsworth, Penguin, 1963), p 107.
4 Ibid, p 111.
5 Proclamation No 25 of 1920, *Laws of South West Africa*, vol 1915–22, p 280.
6 First, *South West Africa*, p 130.

Chapter 4

1 South African Government, *Report on the Natives of South West Africa and Their Treatment by Germany* (London, HMSO, 1918), p 4.
2 C H L Hahn, H Vedder and L Fourie, *Native Tribes of South West Africa* (London, Frank Cass & Co, 1966, first impression 1928), p 162.
3 Richard Freislich, *The Last Tribal War, History of the Bondelswart Uprising in South West Africa, 1922* (Cape Town, C Struik, 1964), p 7.
4 First, *South West Africa*, p 99.
5 Ibid, p 100.
6 Cited in First, *South West Africa*, p 100.
7 See the South African Government's 'Report of the Commission appointed by the Government of the South African Union to inquire into the Rebellion of the Bondelswarts' (1923), U G 16.
8 Cited in Freislich, *Last Tribal War*, p 80.
9 South African Government, 'Report of the Rehoboth Commission' (Cape Town, 1927), presented to both Houses of Parliament by the Governor-General.
10 Cited in First, *South West Africa*, p 100.
11 South African Government, 'Report of the Administrator for 1924', p 25.
12 First, *South West Africa* (Harmondsworth, Penguin, 1963), p 196.
13 Petition to Her Majesty Queen Elizabeth II from Toivo H Ja Toivo and D D Shoombe, Ovamboland People's Congress, 8 May 1958, AB166/4 Rhodes House, Oxford.
14 Ja Toivo, in *Contact* (Cape Town), 13 December 1958.
15 John Ya Otto, *Battlefront Namibia* (London, Heinemann, 1982), p 41.
16 Liberation Support Movement, *Breaking Contract. The Story of Vinnia Ndadi* (Richmond, LSM Press, 1974), p 84.

Chapter 5

1 Cited in Immanuel Geiss, *The Pan-African Movement* (London, Methuen & Co, 1974), p 265.

2   Heinrich Vedder, 'The Herero', in Hahn, Vedder and Fourie, *Native Tribes of SWA*, pp 162–3.
3   Thomas Hodgkin, *Nationalism in Colonial Africa* (New York, New York University Press, 1957), p 84.
4   Negro World, 25 June 1920, cited in G A Pirio, 'The Role of Garveyism in the Making of the Southern African Working Classes and Namibian Nationalism', paper presented to the Conference on 'South Africa and the Comparative Study of Class, Race and Nationalism', New York, 8–12 September 1982, p 29.
5   Ibid, pp 31–2.
6   Ibid, pp 36–7.
7   Zedekia Ngavirue, 'Political Parties and Interest Groups in South West Africa: A Study of a Plural Society', University of Oxford, D Phil thesis, 1972, pp 261–2.
8   John Iliffe, *A Modern History of Tanganyika* (Cambridge, Cambridge University Press, 1979), p 340.
9   J H Wellington, *South West Africa and its Human Issues* (Oxford, Oxford University Press, 1967), p 391. See also M O'Callaghan, *Namibia: The Effects of Apartheid on Culture and Education* (Paris, UNESCO, 1977).
10 See summaries in 'Background paper on new South African laws: Western areas removal scheme', p 2, in L B Greaves, Correspondence on Bantu Education Act of 1953, Mss Afr. s. 922, Rhodes House, Oxford.
11 South African Government, 'Report of the Commission on Native Education 1949–1951', Ref U G No 53/1951, para 924, Pretoria.
12 Statement signed by Simon Petrus-Hoofman, Abram Jacobs, Jakobus Februarie, David Draaier, Isak Jacobs and Hans Swartbooi, AB148/6, Rhodes House, Oxford.
13 Zedekia Ngavirue, 'Political Parties, Organisations and Other Groups in South West Africa 1945–1965', paper presented at the University of Stockholm, Autumn 1965, Part II, p 8.
14 ELOK text read in churches throughout Namibia, 18 July 1971, cited in Mikko Ihamaki, 'Nevertheless, God is Present', *Event* (American Lutheran Church) 14 (2) (1974), pp 38–9.

Chapter 6
1   See the account in Freda Troup, *In Face of Fear: Michael Scott's Challenge to South Africa* (London, Faber, 1950), p 104.
2   Ibid, pp 106–7.
3   Goldblatt, *History of SWA*, p 249.
4   See Troup, *In Face of Fear*, pp 109, 111 and 112.
5   Ibid, p 108.
6   See Ngavirue, 'Political Parties and Interest Groups in SWA', p 245; and First, *South West Africa*, p 181. These communications to the UN can be found in UN Document A/C, 4/37, Annexe 5.
7   UN General Assembly Resolution 65(I), 14 December 1946, see UN Document A/C, 4/37, Annexe 6.
8   Letter from N Hoveka to Stephanus Bingana in Sehitwa, Botswana, 17 June 1946.

9   Troup, *In Face of Fear*, p 147.
10 Ibid, pp 149–50.
11 Michael Scott, *A Time to Speak* (London, Faber, 1958), p 226.
12 First, *South West Africa*, p 182.
13 Scott, *A Time to Speak*, p 235.
14 Ngavirue, 'Political Parties and Interest Groups in SWA', p 243.
15 Letter from Herman Toivo Ja Toivo to Mburumba Kerina, 12 November 1956.
16 One of these men was the late Congressman Allard Lowenstein, who later recounted his experience in *Brutal Mandate: A Journey to South West Africa* (New York, Macmillan, 1962).
17 First, *South West Africa*, p 195.

Chapter 7
1   First, *South West Africa*, p 198.
2   Ibid, p 199.
3   Ibid.
4   Ngavirue, 'Political Parties and Interest Groups in SWA', p 296.
5   Anthony Brian Emmett, 'The Rise of African Nationalism in Namibia/South West Africa 1915–66', University of the Witwatersrand, Johannesburg, MA Dissertation, 1983, p 382.
6   SWANU Constitution.
7   In an inquiry into the Windhoek Shootings of December 1959 (see chapter 8), Kapuuo dissociated himself from SWANU (Ngavirue, 'Political Parties and Interest Groups in SWA', p 300).
8   'Report of the Commission of Enquiry into the Occurrences in the Windhoek Location on the Night of the 10th to the 11th December, 1959, and into the Direct Causes which led to these Occurrences' (Pretoria, 1960) (hereafter the Hall Commission), p 9.
9   First, *South West Africa*, p 201.
10 Ngavirue, 'Political Parties and Interest Groups in SWA', p 303.
11 Cited in Emmett, 'African Nationalism in SWA/Namibia', p 382.
12 Ngavirue, 'Political Parties and Interest Groups in SWA', p 304.
13 SWAPO Constitution.
14 Mburumba Kerina, 'A Brief History of SWAPO', unpublished, July 1960.
15 SWAPO, 'The Programme of the South West Africa People's Organisation', July 1960.

Chapter 8
1   Cited in First, *South West Africa*, p 146.
2   Ibid, p 147.
3   Ngavirue, 'Political Parties and Interest Groups in SWA', p 292.
4   *The Times*, London, 20 December 1959. See also UN General Assembly Resolution 1567(XV) on the Windhoek Location, 18 December 1959.
5   See the Hall Commission.
6   'Deportation! Deportation!', *South West News*, 6 August 1960.
7   Letter from Chiefs Hosea Kutako and Samuel Witbooi, and SWAPO, to the Chairman of the United Nations Committee on

South West Africa, sent c/o the President of Ghana, Accra, 11 June 1961.

8   First, *South West Africa*, p 206.
9   *Freedom* (Cairo, SWANU) II (5–6) (August-September 1964), p 5.
10   Hidipo L Hamutenya and Gottfried Hage Geingob, 'African Nationalism', in C P Potholm and Richard Dale (eds), *Southern Africa in Perspective* (New York, The Free Press, 1972), p 90.
11   See *New Age* (Johannesburg), 27 September 1962; and letters from Jariretundu Kozonguizi, *New Age*, 11 October 1962, and Sam Nujoma, *New Age*, 8 November 1962.
12   *Freedom*, 2 (4) (April-May 1964), p 8.
13   *Freedom*, II (5–6) (August-September 1964), p 10.
14   CANU Constitution.
15   Cited by A J K Kangwa, Under-Secretary for International and Pan-African Affairs of the United National Independence Party (UNIP) of the then newly independent Zambia, in a letter to Mishake Muyongo, 20 July 1965.
16   Emil Appolus, 'September Day Recalled', *Windhoek Observer*, 14 April 1984.
17   See Jariretundu Kozonguizi, 'An Open Letter to the People of Namibia', London, 1 September 1971; 'Kozonguizi – A South African Spy?' (*Windhoek Review*) Yes, this is the evidence', statement refuting allegations against him, 17 October 1969; and 'The Namibian Political Situation', London, December 1971. Also: *Windhoek Review* (Stockholm, SWANU) 1 (4) (May-June 1969) and 1 (5) (July-August 1969).

Chapter 9
1   Ya Otto, *Battlefront Namibia*, p 70.
2   UN General Assembly Resolution 1568 (XV) (18 December 1960).
3   Paul Hare and Herbert Blumberg (eds), *A Search for Peace and Justice: Reflections of Michael Scott* (London, Rex Collings, 1980), p 78.
4   M Hidayatullah, *The South West Africa Case* (London, Asia Publishing House, 1967), p 63.
5   UN General Assembly Official Record, 21st Session, Plenary, 1414th meeting, 23 September 1966, p 9.
6   Iain MacGibbon in Segal and First, *Travesty of Trust*, p 329.
7   United Nations, *A Principle in Torment* (New York, UN, 1971), p 30.
8   UN General Assembly Resolution 2145 (XXV), 27 October 1966.

Chapter 10
1   Andimba Ja Toivo, Statement to the court during the 1967–8 Terrorism Trial in Pretoria, *Trial and Sentencing of Namibians in South Africa* (New York, UN, March 1969), Publications Feature No 8, p 3.
2   SWAPO, Statement of 18 July 1966, Dar es Salaam.
3   Simon Sam Kaukungua, 'Biographical Notes on Tobias Hainyeko', undated.

4   See Ja Toivo's statement extracted under interrogation by the South African police in Pretoria, 27 December 1966, pp 10–13. The statement reveals the extremes to which the South African regime would go to extract information but it also provides a unique picture of SWAPO's early organisation and the events which led to the first clashes between SWAPO fighters and the South African forces.

5   Paul Van Der Merwe, 'South Africa and South West Africa', in Potholm and Dale, *Southern Africa*, p 83.

6   SWAPO, Untitled report on the death of Tobias Hainyeko in 1967.

7   Phillemon was held in detention in Tanzania until 1985 when he was released. He is now living in Norway.

8   The other 33 were: Eliaser Tuhadeleni, John Otto Nankuthu, Simeon Shilungeleni, Julius Israel Shilongo, Lazarus Zachariah, David Hamunime Shimuefeleni, Joseph Helae Shityuvete, Eino Kamati Ekandjo, Festus Nehale, Nghidipo Jesaja Haufiku, Immanuel Augustus Shifidi, Kaleb Tjipahura, Rudolf Kadhikwa, Abel Haluteni, Betuel Nunjango, Michael Ifingilwa Moses, Matias Elia Kanyele, Malakia Shivute Ushona, Johannes Samuel Shiponeni, Petrus Kamati, Matheus Joseph, Jonas Nashivela, Nathaniel Lot Homateni, Phillemon Shitilifa, Simeon Namunganga Hamulemo, Shinima Nailenge, Ndjaula Shaningau, Sakeus Philipus Itika, Ephraim Kamati Kaporo, Simeon Ipinge Iputa, Naftalie Amungulu, Petrus Simon Nilenge, Rehabeam Olavi Nambinga.

9   Ya Otto, *Battlefront Namibia*, pp 94–5.

10 Joel Carlson, *No Neutral Ground* (London, Quartet, 1977), p 92.

11 Ibid, pp 93–4.

12 Ja Toivo's statement to the court, in UN, *Trial and Sentencing of Namibians*.

13 Tuhadeleni's statement to the court, in UN, *Trial and Sentencing of Namibians*.

14 The other 19 were: John Otto Nankuthu, Simeon Shilungeleni, Julius Israel Shilongo, Immanuel Augustus Shifidi, Kaleb Tjipahura, Rudolf Kadhikwa, Abel Haluteni, Betuel Nunjango, Matias Elai Kanyele, Malakia Shivute Ushona, Johannes Samuel Shiponeni, Petrus Kamati, Phillemon Shitilifa, Simeon Namunganga Hamulemo, Shinima Nailenge, Ndjaula Shaningau, Sakeus Philipus Itika, Rehabeam Olavi Nambinga, and Michael Ifingilwa Moses.

15 The other eight were: Lazarus Zachariah, David Hamunime Shimuefeleni, Joseph Helae Shityuvete, Eino Kamati Ekandjo, Festus Nehale, Nghidipo Jesaja Haufiku, Naftalie Amungulu and Petrus Simon Nilenge.

Chapter 11

1   See Vernon Mwaanga, *An Extraordinary Life* (Lusaka, Multimedia Publications, 1982). p 140 ff.

2   International Court of Justice, 'Namibia Opinion (1971)' (The Hague), p 58.

3   South African Administrator in Namibia, Mr Van der Watt, *Cape Times*, 23 June 1971.
4   Kozonguizi, 'Open Letter', September 1971.
5   Colin Winter, *Namibia: the story of a Bishop in Exile* (London, Lutterworth Press, 1977), pp 110–11.
6   Ibid, p 112.
7   Bishop Auala and Moderator Gowaseb, 'Open Letter to His Honour the Prime Minister of South Africa', 30 June 1971, cited in Winter, *Namibia*, pp 113–14. For the full text see also UN Document A/8723. ADD 2.
8   Jan de Wet, cited in the *Windhoek Advertiser*, 16 November 1971.
9   Cited in Winter, *Namibia*, p 118.
10 Gillian and Suzanne Cronje, *The Workers of Namibia* (London, International Defence and Aid Fund for Southern Africa, 1979), p 82.
11 Cited in John Kane-Berman, 'Contract Labour in South West Africa' (Johannesburg, South African Institute of Race Relations, 1972), RR 30/72, appendix III, pp xii-xiii.
12 Winter, *Namibia*, p 119.
13 *Rand Daily Mail*, 1 January 1972, cited in Ray Simons, 'The Namibian Challenge', paper presented to the Namibia International Conference, Brussels, May 1972, p 8.

Chapter 12
1   Absolom L Vilakazi, 'The Odendaal Report: Social and Economic Aspects', in Segal and First, *Travesty of Trust*, p 222.
2   Government of South Africa, 'Report of the Commission of Enquiry into South West Africa Affairs 1962–1963'. The Tomlinson Report of 1951 which set up the Bantustan proposals for South Africa itself was the forerunner of the Odendaal Commission.
3   Vilakazi, 'The Odendaal Report', p 230.
4   For detailed analyses of the Odendaal proposals, see Muriel Horrell, *South West Africa* (Johannesburg, South African Institute of Race Relations, 1967) and Ruth First, 'The Bantustans: The Implications of the Odendaal Report', paper presented to the Namibia International Conference, Brussels, May 1972.
5   Odendaal Report, para 176; and Vilakazi, 'The Odendaal Report', p 220.
6   John Seiler, 'South African Perspectives and Responses to External Pressures', *Journal of Modern African Studies*, 13 (3) (1975), p 462.
7   South African Foreign Minister, Hilgard Muller, *The Star* (Johannesburg), 4 May 1973, cited in J H P Serfontein, *Namibia?* (London, Rex Collings, 1976), p 247.
8   Bishop Winter has written of Kalangula: 'Whether initially he was prompted by motives of personal ambition or had been bribed by the Secret Police, one cannot be sure, but the police used him to spearhead a campaign of violence against my clergy and against the policies that I was attempting to introduce' (*Namibia*, p 67).

Kalangula continued to work within the Bantustan system, first serving as a Minister and currently as Chief Minister in Ovamboland.

9 Gerhard Tötemeyer, *Namibia Old and New* (London, C Hurst, 1978), p 34. The Oniipa ELOK printing press has been destroyed in similar fashion on two occasions since 1973.

10 *Rand Daily Mail*, 17 August 1973.

11 South African Institute of Race Relations, *A Survey of Race Relations in South Africa, 1973* (Johannesburg SAIRR, 1974), p 388.

12 *Rand Daily Mail*, 17 August 1973.

13 Gerhard Tötemeyer and John Seiler, 'South West Africa/Namibia: A Study in Polarization and Confrontation' in John Seiler (ed), *Southern Africa Since the Portuguese Coup* (Boulder, Colorado, Westview Press, 1980), p 86.

14 Tötemeyer, *Namibia Old and New*, p 108.

15 *Namibia News* (London, SWAPO), 8 (3 & 4) March-April 1975, pp 6–7. These reports were corroborated by Amnesty International and the International Commission of Jurists.

16 Cedric Thornberry, 'Report on a visit to Namibia, 18–20 February 1975', summary, p 1.

Chapter 13

1 South African Institute of Race Relations, *Survey of Race Relations 1973*, p 389.

2 Affidavit by Elise Nghiilwamo, Windhoek, 15 March 1974.

3 Bishop Wood was expelled from Namibia in mid-1975 for his part in exposing the floggings.

4 David Soggot, *Namibia: The Violent Heritage* (London, Rex Collings, 1986), p 79.

5 From the official South African tape recordings of the meeting, cited in David Soggot, 'The Struggle for Namibia', unpublished MS, 1982, p 123.

6 Soggot, *Namibia: The Violent Heritage*, p 83.

7 Cited in Soggot, *Namibia: The Violent Heritage*, p 89.

8 Ibid, pp 90–1.

9 Ibid, p 94.

10 Ibid, p 95.

11 Ibid, p 99.

12 Affidavit by Axel Johannes, Gobabis, 15 August 1974.

13 Cedric Thornberry, 'Report, 22–29 August 1975', p 2.

14 Nkandi then went into exile. Although Johannes is also now in exile, he stayed in Namibia until 1982 and suffered further spells of imprisonment and torture – being buried alive at one stage – although he was never found guilty of any crime. He has become one of the symbols of Namibian nationalist resistance.

15 Soggot, *Namibia: The Violent Heritage*, p 157.

16 Ibid, p 161.

17 Cited in Soggot, *Namibia: The Violent Heritage*, p 162.

18 Cedric Thornberry, 'Report on a visit to Namibia, 30 October-3 November 1974'.

Chapter 14

1 Mao Tse Tung, *Selected Works* (London, Lawrence & Wishart, 1954), vol 1,p 124.

2 Interview conducted by the author with one of SWAPO's early field commanders, Rahimisa Kahimise, Oxford, 27 July 1984.

3 *Rand Daily Mail*, 14 October 1968, cited in the South African Institute of Race Relations, *A Survey of Race Relations in South Africa, 1968* (Johannesburg, SAIRR, 1969), p 64.

4 *The Star* (Johannesburg), 29 May 1971.

5 The irony of the Angolan situation is that as future events developed UNITA and SWAPO were pitted directly against each other. A long and bitter war has been fought between the MPLA and UNITA since 1975, with UNITA being assisted by South Africa. In return for this support, UNITA has been required by South Africa to attack SWAPO. Now SWAPO military units will also attack UNITA units when they encounter them.

6 *Namibia News* (London, SWAPO), 4 (3–10) (March-October 1971), p 2.

7 *Namibia News*, 7 (6 & 7) (June-July 1974), p 2.

8 English translation of South African army document in Afrikaans, SWA/T1/552/1, June 1984, marked Secret, 'Minutes of the Security Conference held at Windhoek 17–18 May 1984', p E.

9 *Sunday Times* (Johannesburg), 10 February 1980, cited in International Defence & Aid Fund, *Apartheid's Army in Namibia* (London, IDAF, 1982), Fact Paper No 10, p 13.

10 SWAPO, Press statement by Peter Nanyemba, Secretary for Defence, at a press conference in Luanda, 15 April 1980.

11 Interview with Greenwell Matongo, Political Commissar of PLAN (London, October 1977). Part of this interview has been reproduced in *Namibia Today* (Lusaka, SWAPO), 1 (3) (1977).

12 *Africa Confidential* (London), 7 September 1973.

13 IDAF, *Apartheid's Army in Namibia*, p 13.

14 Ibid, pp 16–18 and note 5 for futher details.

15 Ibid, p 11.

16 Southern African Catholic Bishops' Conference (1982) pp 20–1, cited by Gavin Cawthra, *Brutal Force: The Apartheid War Machine* (London, International Defence & Aid Fund, 1986), p 212.

17 Cited in *The Independent*, London, 1 April 1987.

18 Peter Nanyemba/SWAPO Military Council, 'The Launching of an Armed Struggle was the Necessity to Liberate Our People from Colonial Bondage and to Regain Our Fatherland', undated discussion paper (early 1970s).

19 Liberation Support Movement, Interview with PLAN Political Commissar Kokauru Nganjone, *Namibia: SWAPO Fights for Freedom* (Oakland. California, LSM Press, 1978), p 40.

20 Liberation Support Movement, Interview with SWAPO Secretary for Information and Publicity, Andreas Shipanga, *Interviews in Depth – Namibia, SWAPO, 1* (Richmond, Canada, LSM Press, 1973), p 14.

21 Interview with Kahimise.
22 LSM, Interview with Nganjone, p 44.
23 Interview with Kahimise.

Chapter 15
1   Constitution of the National Convention, translated from Afrikaans.
2   UN General Assembly Resolution 3111, 12 December 1973.
3   Chief Clemens Kapuuo, Statement, Windhoek, 7 January 1975.
4   Namibia National Convention, 'Annual Report' 1975, p 1.
5   International Defence and Aid Fund for Southern Africa, 'All Options and None: The Constitutional Talks in Namibia' (London, IDAF, August 1976), Fact Paper No 3.
6   Namibia National Convention, 'The NNC on Present-Day Namibia', Windhoek, 30 May 1975.
7   SWAPO, 'Discussion Paper on the Constitution of Independent Namibia', 1976, 4th Revise, para 37.
8   Ibid, para 42.
9   IDAF, 'All Options and None', p 4.
10 See the statement by Arnold I Burns before the Sub-Committee on International Organisations of the Committee on International Relations of the United States House of Representatives, on 27 August 1976.
11 UN Security Council, Resolution 385, adopted at its 1885th meeting, on 30 January 1976.
12 Statement signed by Pastor H Witbooi, Mr J Stefanus, Mr S Isaks and Mr H Noeteb, Windhoek, October 1976.
13 UN General Assembly Resolution 31/146, adopted at its 105th plenary session on 20 December 1976.
14 Ibid.
15 Statement to the Windhoek Observer by Miss Kurundiro Kapuuo, a niece of Chief Kapuuo.
16 Justin Ellis, Elections in Namibia? (London, British Council of Churches and Catholic Institute for International Relations, 1979).
17 See Agence France Presse and Die Suidwester, 7 December 1978, cited in Ellis, Elections in Namibia?, p 29.

Chapter 16
1   SWAPO, 'The Verbatim Record of the Second Annual General Conference of the Executive National Committee of the South West Africa People's Organisation', held at the External Headquarters, Dar es Salaam, on 15 June 1965.
2   SWAPO 'Resolutions' adopted at the Consultative Congress of SWAPO in Tanga, Tanzania, 26 December 1969 – 2 January 1970.
3   SWAPO, 'Report of the Findings and Recommendations of the John Ya Otto Commission of Inquiry into Circumstances which led to the Revolt of SWAPO Cadres between June 1974 and April 1976', 4 June 1976, Lusaka, p 9.

4   Ibid, p 11.
5   Ibid, p 1.
6   The others were: Nathaniel Pelao Keshii, SYL President; Reuben Sheeli Shangula, SYL Secretary General; Jimmy Amupala, SYL Executive Committee member; Immanuel Engombe, SYL Executive Committee member; Filemon Moongo, SYL Executive Committee member; Andreas Nuukwawo, SYL Executive Committee member; Sakaria Shikomba, Research officer in SWAPO's Department of Information; Martin Taneni, PLAN fighter; and Ndeshi Uyumba (the only woman among the eleven), SYL Executive Committee member.
7   SWAPO, Ya Otto Commission, p 4.
8   SWAPO Democrats, 'Basic Documents'.
9   SWAPO, *Political Programme* (Lusaka, SWAPO, 1977), p 6.
10 Ibid, p 12.
11 Oxfam-Canada Program Development Officers, *Reports from Southern Africa*, II (2) (November 1978).
12 Dr Libertine Amathila, cited in Oxfam-Canada, *Reports from Southern Africa*.
13 People's Republic of Angola, *White Paper on Acts of Aggression by the Racist South African Regime against the People's Republic of Angola, 1975–1982* (Luanda, 1983), III, p 15. This was presented at the UN General Assembly Session in 1983.
14 Ibid.
15 Cited in the *Johannesburg Sunday Times*, 7 May 1978.
16 SWAPO Women's Council, 'Namibian Women in the Struggle for National Liberation, Independence and Reconstruction', UNESCO Regional Experts Meeting on 'The History of Women's Contribution to National Liberation Struggles and Their Roles and Needs During Reconstruction in Newly Independent Countries of Africa', Bissau, Guinea-Bissau, 3–7 September 1983, UNESCO Document SS-83/CONF. 619/6, Paris, 9 June 1983, p 27 and note 40.
17 Ibid, p 2.
18 Ibid, p 3.
19 Elizabeth Landis and Michael Davis, 'Namibia: Impending Independence?' in Gwendolen M Carter and Patrick O'Meara (eds), *Southern Africa. The Continuing Crisis* (Basingstoke, Macmillan, 1979), p 15.

Chapter 17

1   Cyrus Vance, *Hard Choices. Critical Years in America's Foreign Policy* (New York, Simon and Schuster, 1983), p 276.
2   Ibid, p 277.
3   Confidential note handed to the officials of the South African government in Cape Town on 27–29 April 1977, by the Contact Group, para 3B.
4   Ibid, para 3E.
5   Internal report dated 13 May 1977 from SWAPO Deputy National Chairman Daniel Tjongarero, on SWAPO's meeting with representatives of the Contact Group on the Cape Town talks of 9 May 1977.

6   Ibid.
7   SWAPO reply to the note from representatives of the Contact Group, Lusaka, 27 May 1977.
8   Vance, *Hard Choices*, p 278.
9   Ibid, p 279.
10 Ibid, p 281.
11 SWAPO, 'Proposals for a Negotiated Settlement in Namibia', 24 July 1977, Lusaka. Paper presented to the Contact Group in their August 1977 meeting with SWAPO.
12 The Contact Group, Internal report (untitled) on negotiations after their meeting with SWAPO in early August 1977, para 12.
13 Ibid, para 6.
14 Ibid, para 10.
15 Vance, *Hard Choices*, p 279.
16 Ibid, p 283.
17 Ibid, p 303.
18 Ibid, p 305.
19 Ibid, p 306.
20 UN Security Council Resolution 431, 27 July 1978.
21 UN Security Council Resolution 432, 27 July 1978.

Chapter 18

1   UN Security Council Document S/12827, 29 August 1978. 'Report of the Secretary-General Submitted Pursuant to Paragraph 2 of Security Council Resolution 431 (1978) Concerning the Situation in Namibia'.
2   Letter from SWAPO President Sam Nujoma to UN Secretary-General Kurt Waldheim, 8 September 1978, commenting on the Secretary-General's report on implementation of the Contact Group's proposals.
3   Letter from the South African Minister of Foreign Affairs, R F Botha, to the UN Secretary-General Kurt Waldheim on the Secretary-General's Report on Implementation of the Contact Group's Proposals, 6 September 1978. Issued to the press by the South African Mission to the UN, New York.
4   Ibid.
5   Statement on Namibia by the South African Prime Minister, B J Vorster, 20 September 1978, Pretoria.
6   France was represented by its Minister of State for Foreign Affairs.
7   Interview with Dr David Owen, former British Foreign Secretary (1976–9), London, 16 January 1985.
8   Ellis, *Elections in Namibia?*, p 15.
9   UN Security Council Resolution 439 of 13 November 1978.
10 Vance, *Hard Choices*, p 310.
11 See UN Security Council Document S/13143, 6 March 1979. 'Letter dated 6 March 1979 from the Chargé d'Affaires of the Permanent Mission of South Africa to the United Nations addressed to the Secretary-General'. Covering the text of a

statement by the South African Prime Minister, P W Botha, in the House of Assembly, Cape Town, on Namibia.

12 Ibid, plus communication outlining 'SWAPO's Comments and Recommendations to the UN Secretary-General on the Implementation of the UN Plan', 10 February 1979, Luanda.

13 'SWAPO's Comments and Recommendations to the UN Secretary-General', 10 February 1979, Luanda.

14 Statement by South African Administrator General in Namibia, Danie Hough, at the Pre-Implementation Meeting, 13 January 1981. For further details of the meeting, see *Documentation on the UN Pre-Implementation Meeting on Namibia, Geneva, January 7–14, 1981* (Geneva, Lutheran World Federation). See also D Geldenhuys, *The Diplomacy of Isolation: South African Foreign Policy Making* (Johannesburg, Macmillan, for the South African Institute of International Affairs, 1984), p 230.

15 Foreign and Commonwealth Office, 'Namibia: Progress Towards Independence' (London, May 1984, Background Brief Series), p 3.

16 UN Security Council Document S/15287, 12 July 1982. 'Letter dated 12 July 1982 from the Representatives of Canada, France, Federal Republic of Germany, the United Kingdom of Great Britain and Northern Ireland and the United States of America addressed to the Secretary-General'. Covering 'Principles Concerning the Constituent Assembly and the Constitution for an Independent Namibia'.

17 Announced by the French Foreign Minister, Claud Cheysson, in the French Parliament on 7 December 1983.

18 Foreign and Commonwealth Office, 'Namibia: Progress Towards Independence' (London, May 1984, Background Brief Series), p 3.

INDEX

144